COMMENTS ON WENDY EVANS AS A WRITER, SPEAKER, TRAINER AND CONSULTANT.

'I congratulate Wendy Evans on an exceptional book. Every page is convincing. All the points made are easily taken on board and clearly expressed. The book develops the art of persistence into fine-tuned skills. Chapter by chapter, fears are systematically changed into formulas for business success.'
—**Dr. Henry Nowik, Distinguished Research Professor, Georgetown University, Washington, D.C.**

'Wendy Evans' concept and approach to our project (as a new division of Johnson & Johnson) was right on target. She helped us design a direct marketing lead generation campaign to build awareness of our products. Wendy did an outstanding job.'
—**Donna Conforti, Product Director Johnson and Johnson HMI, USA.**

'Wendy Evans took full responsibility for our marketing activities and promotional material. She developed a target list of 8000 names whom we contacted every 90 days with telemarketing follow-up for appointment setting. In the execution of this she excelled. We credit Wendy with our entrepreneurial success.'
—**Marshall Jeanes, Vice Chairman, IMCOR, New York.**

'I found myself getting excited as I read, thinking, "Yes, yes, this is what we need for the plans we have for K. Mart".'
—**Bob Dalziel, Managing Director, K. Mart, Australia.**

'What a great piece of writing! For the first time I found a book that takes the mystique out of marketing. This book will be of immense value to both the experienced marketing specialist and the uninitiated. It makes easy reading and presents stimulating and illuminating information. I had difficulty in putting the book down.'
—**Ron Mantel, School of Tourism and Hospitality,**
Cornell University/Canberra Institute of Technology, Australia.

'Exceptional material, exceptionally well presented. And best of all the skills can be put into practice immediately.'
—**Klaus Reincke, Vice President,**
Royal Abjar Hotel Group. United Arab Emirates.

'We believed you, Wendy. You have credibility that comes from your soul. It is like finding a diamond in the desert.'
—**Sales staff, Bristol Myers Squibb, South Africa.**

'So nice to be given a workshop by someone who has been there and relates the experiences in simple, realistic terms. No frills, no special tricks, no complicated methods. A very refreshing experience.'
—**Sales Staff, 3M, South Africa.**

'Thank you for your most entertaining, informative and helpful seminar. The feedback has been wonderful. We very much appreciated your gift of time, wisdom and enthusiasm.'
—**Barbara Rogers, President, Financial Women's Association, New York.**

'*Choose and Grow your Own Business in 90 Days* is a book for today. It is an eminently useful, sensible and well-written book with compelling information. Choose what you want to do with passion, and use that passion to thrive and prosper.'
Sir Clement Freud, London.

choose & grow *your own* BUSINESS (IN) 90 DAYS

Wendy Evans

NEW HOLLAND

Published in Australia in 1999 by
New Holland Publishers (Australia) Pty Ltd
Sydney • Auckland • London • Cape Town
14 Aquatic Drive Frenchs Forest NSW 2086 Australia
218 Lake Road Northcote Auckland New Zealand
24 Nutford Place London W1H 6DQ United Kingdom
80 McKenzie Street Cape Town 8001 South Africa

First published in 1999 and reprinted in 1999

National Library of Australia
Cataloguing-in-Publication Data:
Evans, Wendy, 1940–.
Choose and grow your own business in 90 days.

Includes index.
ISBN 1 86436 437 8.

1 Small business — Management. 2. Marketing.
3. New business enterprises — Management. I. Title.

658.022

Editors: Catherine Hammond and Julie Nekich
Designer: Peta Nugent
Typesetter: Post Pre-press Group, Brisbane
Printed in Australia by Griffin Press

DEDICATION

To all the companies I have worked with,
their managers and their staff, in the following countries:
Australia
Hong Kong
Singapore
Malaysia
Thailand
China
United Kingdom
United States of America
South Africa
New Zealand
United Arab Emirates:
Dubai, Abu Dhabi, Dohar and Oman.

Without your trust, support and invitations to speak,
train and consult, there would never have been
anything to write home about.

THANK YOU

To David Miln of Saatchi & Saatchi, London, because you were always there to share, discuss, argue and feed my zeal. And even bought the book!
To Stuart and Sue Sanders, Sanders Consulting, Richmond, Virginia, USA, for training me in their new-business modules. Their work appears here in the sections on the four main personality styles. Nowhere else have I met such dedication to the business of doing new business well.
I am proud to have known you and worked with you.
To Robert Byrne, from whose excellent collection of quotations I drew: *1,911 Best Things Anybody Ever Said*, Fawcett Columbine, New York, 1988. This book is a great read and gave me endless hours of fun in choosing the quotes.
To all who commented on and added to my on-the-job studies; they number in the thousands now, and some appear in this book as case studies.
To my many friends, whose support and nourishment have kept me going over these many years of travel. This great band includes Sir Clement Freud—for his help and guidance in London, and Nancy Rodrigues, Wendy Braund, Jo Kaufmann and Helen Barr—for their care in typing and editing for me, for supporting and enchanting me in New York. To Ros and Ian Hurrell and Ann Blunt in Sydney, who were an endless source of fun and support, taking me out of my writer's den and into their family and homes and the joys of Sydney living.
To Patricia and Peter Sweatman in Melbourne, who have single-mindedly cared for me, entertained me, re-addressed mail endlessly, stored numerous items and looked after my business affairs with never a murmur of complaint.

CONTENTS

CONTENTS

INTRODUCTION

This book is for all of you who have ever thought, 'I want to start my own business, but I don't know what to do.' You have said it often, too, in seminars and workshops. Thank you for that, because you encouraged me into a rich and interesting journey of discovery on just how to choose a business wisely and well.

First I thought about the people I knew who were successful in their own business—and happy and well balanced in it.

This is what I found they had in common:

One: They were doing something they loved to do; they had a passion that drove them.

Two: They were happy to serve others; they were not trying to make a killer sale on the spot. Rather they preferred to learn whether or not they could **help** the prospect or client. If they could, they were quietly persistent until they were needed. If not, they moved on until another time.

Three: They planned to be successful. They lived their business plans and their marketing plans and managed their finances well. They shared and updated their goals and plans with their staff and families, they researched clients and their families constantly to learn how they could do things better together. And they listened.

They listened to their staff, their families and their clients. Then when they understood the issues, they responded. They hired the right people for the right job. They gave their people the training and the systems to do it right. Does this sound like the way you would run your business?

Shortly you are going to do a simple test to see if you are the right personality to be an entrepreneur. Or are you better

'There is only one thing about which I am certain and that is that there is very little about which one can be certain.'
W. Somerset
Maugham
(1874–1965)

suited to be a franchisee? What is your passion and how can you turn it into a successful business? The answers are coming. But first, an overview of the twelve Growth Skills that will provide you with practical knowledge to develop valuable business growth, whether you are starting up or wanting to expand.

GROWTH SKILL ONE:

Stay in touch within 90 days. Three is the proven number; make contact with your prospects within three months. We seem to know innately that 'three' is the way to go. Don't seasons have three months? Don't we say, 'Third time lucky' and 'Try, try, try again'? New-business activities must be ongoing over the life of your company, not on a stop-start-stop basis. Proven by Saatchi & Saatchi over a 20-year test period and during my time with Inter-Continental Hotels, 90 days, or less, is the cycle for building relationships.

'How much money did you make last year? Mail it in.'
Simplified tax form suggested by Stanton Delaplane

GROWTH SKILL TWO:

To grow your business you need both hunters and farmers. Hunters need to be out and about, chasing up the business. These are the 'high energy' people.

One type of high energy person has little regard for detail and finances, but enormous vision of what could be, so this person functions better as the head of a large, rich corporation.

The other type is more the entrepreneur, with that tenacious desire to succeed—and they do. Hire this personality for your sales development.

The quieter, low-energy people are your farmers. The detail-oriented accountant and the soft, gentle human resources person will readily care for your business, but never ask them for a sales role.

Hire the people you need in the roles that suit them. To make it easy, I have included a personality profile test that will ensure you are close to right every time.

'Only the mediocre are always at their best.'
Jean Giraudoux (1882–1994)

GROWTH SKILL THREE:

Build a wide band of well-chosen prospects through the commonality survey. Sales people can all too often be choking the life out of too few prospects. Don't get caught up in pursuing only 20 prospects when you can be gently nudging 200 or more.

You will likely have had the experience yourself of being hotly pursued and then dumped if you did not obey the demand to buy their product, **now**.

Don't let that sense of being held by the throat apply to your prospects. People don't mean 'no', they mean 'not now'. What is important is that you are still there when it is the right time for them to buy.

Good new prospects can look very like your current excellent clients. The Commonality Survey section will help you find your future best prospects by looking at the common elements of your current best clients.

Of likely key importance is their proximity to your place of business, your understanding of their product or service and their reliability (or not) in paying their bills.

Beyond that, your greatest success will come from the people whom you understand, respect and enjoy being with.

I stress proximity because it is the same in business as with your friends: you see more of the ones nearby than those across the river, over the railway line, out of town.

When people feel near to you, they are more likely to phone you, drop by, give you business. Moreover, the cost of doing business is less on both sides.

GROWTH SKILL FOUR:

The single-minded proposition. You must know what it is, quite simply, that your company provides, from the client's point of view. With the 'single-minded proposition' finalised, you can then create an umbrella statement for all your future corporate communications.

Without it, you have no guidelines with which to brief your advertising, PR, sales promotion and direct marketing staff or agencies. Again, if you are just beginning to think about starting your own business, do this exercise for competitors' businesses until you get it right for yours.

Start by asking what it is that your favourite store, restaurant, hotel, or car provides for you. This has nothing to do with the obvious statements like 'provides clothing/food/a bed to sleep in/a mode of getting around the place'.

It has everything to do with courteous service, a great atmosphere, value for money, and the feel of the power and the wind in your hair. A sense of wanting more.

GROWTH SKILL FIVE:

'It is only possible to live happily ever after on a day-to-day basis.' **Margaret Bonnano**

Look like the company you want to be. Make your entity enticing to staff, prospects and clients. Use design and colour to make your company look solid and stable or new and exciting. The image your company conveys by its decor and written materials is received in a split second.

Research around the world shows that people like to buy from men dressed in the Dunhill look: navy blue blazer, crisp white shirt and a red-and-blue-striped tie. Trousers can be grey or camel, shoes can be slip-on or lace-up. Socks have to match the shoes.

The world likes to buy from women dressed in white, black, black and white, navy, navy and white, and royal blue and white. Discreet make-up and jewellery, and carefully applied lipstick are also noticed. (To make sure your lipstick is not sticking to your teeth, pull your middle finger through your pursed lips.)

Skirts can be above the knee but not too short, shoes low heeled, preferably black with relatively sheer black stockings. Hair must be tidy and clean. No perfume—tests show that the perfume you love is the one someone else hates or is allergic to. **Message: keep the fun stuff for nights and weekends.**

'I base my fashion on what doesn't itch.'
Gilda Radner

GROWTH SKILL SIX:

Success in your calling cycles. Your 'sound' is important, too. If you heard yourself or your staff live on radio in your daily dealings with clients, suppliers and prospects, would you be pleased and proud?

Try this simple activity: leave your office and go to the office of an understanding business acquaintance with a speaker phone. Listen while your friend rings your office and asks for you/wants to leave a message/wants the fax number/asks even for your home number.

See if your staff are pleasant and courteous or offhanded and rushed. Then again, have that same friend pose as a buyer of your product or service and see what sort of response the staff feels competent to give.

GROWTH SKILL SEVEN:

Defend your right to be absolutely consistent in your corporate messages—even to the point of boring yourself (but not others). Keep your regular follow-up messages the same, endlessly. Do not confuse your listener/viewer with new sounds, new colours, new messages.

Why be boring? Why not? Coca-Cola is probably boring to

the people who work there and to the advertisers at times, but to us, the consumers, it is endlessly the same in its logo and sexy fun image. We know and love Coca-Cola.

We know and love McDonald's, Kentucky Fried Chicken and Pizza Hut, too, and I love the Regent Hotels with a passion—not because they advertise endlessly, but because they behave in the same stupendously excellent way wherever I am lucky enough to experience them.

GROWTH SKILL EIGHT:

Sales promotion. Create and maintain a competitive edge. When people see something they like, they rationalise the buying decision through fear, greed and laziness. Feed the greed.

'The biggest sin is sitting on your ass.'
Florynce Kennedy

Maintain a competitive edge by making effective and continuous special offers to move product and bring forward the purchase decision in your favour. Be flexible, be understanding of the other person's needs and wants, put them ahead of your own. Then you win, too.

Think back to your experiences in purchasing and contracting for major items, like a house, a car, furniture, additions to your home. Recall the experience of signing these purchase orders or business contracts for employment, premises, equipment, whatever.

Think what it would have been like if all the transactions had been friendly and courteous. You were spending a lot of money, almost putting your life on the line, and wouldn't it have been great if they had acknowledged that by offering some relevant gift to mark the occasion?

Imagine if they had sat down with you to look at the contract together and invited you to comment on anything that caused you concern! Then suppose they had expressed their willingness to cooperate—and meant it!

GROWTH SKILL NINE:

Self management. How to keep yourself organised. We cannot, of course, manage time. It does its own thing. But we can manage ourselves. Remember, nobody ever died wishing they had spent more time in the office—or in my opinion, cooking dinners and washing up.

Be organised. All the other growth skills will be of no use if you're unable to manage your day. One of the best tips I have come across in time management is to divide the number of projects you have on your desk by the number of minutes in your working day.

If you have fifty projects, you can give each eight minutes. You can make a lot of decisions and shift a lot of 'monkeys' off your back in that time, as well as go to lunch.

If you are a solo operator or running a business with few staff, you can find you have too many things to do, all the time. Try to do whatever is relatively **unimportant** first, so that these things never become important. These things take on a life of their own when ignored.

Do a few of these 'unimportant' things every day, and they will never become a major issue. They will just flow on as part of your processes each morning.

Manage your time to be effective. Understand the difference between 'important' and 'urgent'. Beware of people who rush in and interrupt your work to push their 'urgent' work onto you. It might be urgent for them, but perhaps it is important for you to keep on with your tasks. If you stop to help them, will you stop being effective for yourself?

Do a business plan for your business with all your staff understanding their key objectives. Manage your time to meet those objectives. Anything that takes you or your staff away

'Wagner's music is better than it sounds.'
Bill Nye (1850–1896)

from meeting those goals is potentially damaging to the health and success of your business. Say no, from a position of strength.

GROWTH SKILL TEN:

Understand your staff, clients and prospects by understanding yourself in terms of your personality and your personal communications style. Some people are magic to deal with, others awkward. When you understand yourself, you understand what is going on around you.

I set out to understand others, to adapt, to find the right words for their needs. In my personal relationships I expect people to behave exactly the way they are. I try not to push the buttons that will upset them, or to get upset myself because they are not like me. Life is unbelievably easier.

GROWTH SKILL ELEVEN:

Plan to succeed. You must have a set of goals with actions and costs for the future, a strategic plan by which to guide your business and promotional plans for your individual product or service.

'If you are not beguiling by the age of 12, forget it.'
Lucy (Charles Schultz)

This can easily be achieved by this simple technique. You can see the future by standing there and looking backwards from there to today.

Start with that end in mind and write your marketing and business plans accordingly. Where do you want to be in a few years' time? What actions do you need to take to make it happen?

A friend of mine used to say, 'Beware of what you want, for you shall surely get it.' Just sitting down and thinking your way through the actions for success will generate that success. Then write down these actions, timing and costs, to 'carve them in stone' and commit yourself to action.

To be successful as a business, you must have:

- Good product
- Good marketing
- Good financial management

backed up with passion, planning and persistence.

Will you/do you have all this?

GROWTH SKILL TWELVE:

Through case studies, learn how these skills fit together and what they have done for companies big and small. Read about and learn from the simple growth skills that made my clients great around the world.

Remember, there are three ways to grow your business:

- Grow your client base
- Grow the frequency of purchase
- Grow your profit by better management of your costs and/or increasing your prices.

Plan to do all three to grow and succeed.

Three things to remember about being persistent, regularly and relentlessly:

'You get what you focus on.' **Anthony Robbins**

One: When people say 'no', they usually mean 'not now', if you have carefully chosen them as prospects. If, on the other hand, you have grabbed a whole lot of names at random, they may well mean 'no'.

Two: When they say 'no', they say it to the opportunity, not to you.

Three: If you do not want to make those phone calls and are finding all sorts of excuses, it is because you believe that the prospects on the other end are saying 'no' to you, not to the opportunity. But you have got it the wrong way around.

Just a small change in your way of thinking and you really will stop caring about rejection.

Now for the test. Are you best suited to be an entrepreneur or should you be a franchisee instead? Know your passions so that you will be successful through doing the things you love to do.

ENTREPRENEUR OR FRANCHISEE?

This part of the book is all about your passion: the passion to be in business for yourself, doing something that you are passionate about; the passion to go out there and get and keep profitable clients.

Before committing yourself to being an entrepreneur of any type, the most important question of all is: do you have what it takes?

The Entrepreneurial Test

The following test is written as if you are still an employee. If you have already started your own business, just answer as if you were still in your last job.

Put a ring around your honest answer. Add up your score using the number beside the letter of your answer. The test helps you decide if the entrepreneurial life is for you, so answer as you are, not as you wish you could be.

■ ■ ■

Obviously, the higher the score, the more likely you are to relish the entrepreneurial life, but certain questions are really important, such as, 'Do you really want to own your own business?' and 'Do you feel you can shape your own destiny?'

Think long and hard before committing yourself to owning your own business if your answer to these two is 'no'.

'Mathematics has given economics rigor, but alas also mortis.'
Robert Heilbroner

THE ENTREPRENEURIAL PROFILE TEST

1. Does your family stand by you in everything you undertake?
   A 4 Yes *(circled)*
   B 1 No
   C 2 Sometimes

2. Do you carry out less pleasant tasks first, even though you would rather do something else?
   A 4 Yes *(circled)*
   B 1 No
   C 3 Most of the time

3. Are you organised and methodical in your work?
   A 4 Yes *(circled)*
   B 1 No
   C 3 Most of the time
   D 2 Occasionally

4. Does it frustrate you if you are unable to buy the things you want?
   A 4 Yes
   B 1 No
   C 2 Not often
   D 3 Quite often *(circled)*

5. Can you find anything you want in your work-place in around three minutes?
   A 4 Yes
   B 1 No *(circled)*

6. Are you/were you happy in your current job?
   A 2 Yes
   B 3 No *(circled)*

7. Do you achieve best when you have someone managing and directing you?
   A 1 Yes
   B 4 No *(circled)*
   C 2 Most of the time

8. As an employee did you/do you keep your head down and get on with it, or do you suggest new ideas at various levels?

   A 1 Make no suggestions

   B 4 Always suggesting changes

   C 3 Quite often suggest changes

   D 2 Hardly ever make suggestions

9. Does being in a noisy office, cramped working conditions or a poor neighbourhood prevent you from achieving?

   A 1 Can do so

   B 3 Don't notice

10. Do you want your own business?

   A 4 Absolutely

   B 0 Not at all

   C 3 Only if I can come up with a totally secure idea

   D 1 Thinking about it

11. Do you handle personal finances well?

   A 4 Yes, carefully and diligently at all times

   B 1 No, I am useless

   C 3 Most of the time

   D 2 I try every so often but find it
        difficult to live within a budget

12. How seriously do you take your mistakes at work, even if you are only partly to blame?

   A 3 Very seriously

   B 1 Lose little sleep over them

13. Are you a people person?

   A 3 Yes

   B 1 No

   C 2 Yes, in small doses

THE ENTREPRENEURIAL PROFILE TEST

14. Do you plan your work *and* personal life?
    - A1 No, not at all.
    - B4 Yes, always
    - C2 Seldom
    - D3 If it seems important

15. Is the money you could make the primary reason for contemplating your own business?
    - A2 Yes
    - B3 No

16. How flexible are you in your work day? If things become difficult do you adapt and complete the task?
    - A1 No, I down tools
    - B4 Yes, I adapt readily
    - C2 I am a little flexible depending on the circumstances

17. Do you feel you can truly shape your own destiny?
    - A4 Yes
    - B1 No

18. Do you like taking risks and calculated gambles?
    - A4 Yes
    - B1 No
    - C2 If the odds are in my favour

19. Do you keep your head in a crisis?
    - A4 Yes
    - B1 No
    - C3 Depends on the crisis

20. If there were plenty of good jobs, would you still want your own business?
    - A4 Yes
    - B1 No

with thanks to ABSA

Let's say, you've passed the test, you are a committed entrepreneur, you have money and skills. Now you need to know how you can be successful day in and day out. Like anything else, this is about a set of rules and skills, and if you abide by them, then 'luck' is on your side. The rules are called the 'three threes to success'. Get these right and you will have a thriving business.

RULE NUMBER ONE:

You must have:

- Good product
- Good marketing
- Good financial management.

(If any one of these is missing, the business will not succeed. Each one of the three is as important as the other.)

RULE NUMBER TWO:

The three ways to grow your business are:

- Grow your client base
- Grow the frequency of purchase
- Grow your profit through increasing your prices and/or better managing your costs.

RULE NUMBER THREE:

The three reasons people buy (after they have seen something they like):

- Greed
- Fear
- Laziness

'Why is there so much month left at the end of the money?'
Unknown

And these rules for success have to be backed up with passion, planning and persistence. Starting now, you will learn how to make these rules work for you, to choose a business and grow a business.

How do the 'three threes' help you choose a business?
Imagine you are going to buy an existing business and you use the above 'three threes' as a guideline.

For instance, does this business have good product, good marketing and good financial management? If the answer to even one of those is negative, then the business is sure to fail—and that missing link may well be the reason it is being sold.

Do not proceed unless you have the resources to patch the business up.

If all is well, go on to the next set of threes. Can this company be grown through:

(a) growing the client base

(b) growing the frequency of purchase

(c) increasing the profit by putting up the prices and/or managing the costs better?

> 'Income tax has made more liars out of people than golf and fishing.'
> **Jim Stone**

If the answer is yes to all three, continue. If no to any, stop and think long and hard.

Will this product or service lend itself to being promoted through pushing the buttons of

(a) greed

(b) fear and

(c) laziness/busyness/tiredness—whatever?

Example: friend Linda lived in a cold house and was determined to get out before the next winter. She saw the house she liked (it faced the morning sun and had underfloor heating). So her fear of cold would be taken care of. The price was right, so that met the greed need. If she signed for the house then and there, she could get on with her life (laziness/boredom/busyness—call it what you will).

Next her car broke down, yet again. She saw the car she really wanted and the offer on the trade-in was good (greed), she was due to go out of town on a business trip so needed a reliable car (fear), and if she said yes she could get on with earning money to pay for both major purchases (laziness/busyness/boredom—whatever). When I saw her the other day, she was the top-selling sales person in her company. She said fear of the outstanding debt drove her!

Don proved this fear, greed and laziness concept, too. His wife rang to say that his favourite men's wear shop was having a sale and he was **not** to come home without some new clothes. He went immediately to the shop (fear of wife), found the sale was 50 per cent off (greed) and bought so many clothes that he will not have to shop again until the year 2005 (laziness in the extreme).

> 'Business is a good game. Lots of competition and a minimum of rules. You keep score with money.'
> **Atari founder, Nolan Bushnell**

Will you be able to promote your new business using this concept? Think about how many things you have bought in the last few years which were justified by a discount or a free gift, by being too busy to look further, or by fear that someone else would grab it if you didn't.

Realise that if you don't have the price flexibility to make special offers, you may end up with lots of sightseers and little or no commitment to buy.

A client said recently that we probably even get married for greed, fear and laziness: greed, because the prospect looks like he/she will earn/inherit good money; fear that if you don't grab him or her someone else will; and laziness, for if you marry, you won't have to go out on another date.

Of course we call it love, but that's the icing on the cake!

FOLLOW YOUR PASSION TO CHOOSE YOUR BUSINESS

The first and most important commandment is: follow your passion, preferably a passion for something that the marketplace already understands. Why? Because life is too short and money in too short supply to enforce the understanding of a brand new product. It is far easier and far better to have a passion for something the whole world wants and already knows that it wants. Add a little twist, a new benefit, and the world will understand immediately.

> 'We can't all be heroes because somebody has to sit on the curb and clap as they go by.'
> **Will Rogers**
> **(1879–1935)**

Finding that passion

A client said she had no passion, yet she wanted to be her own boss. After much probing she admitted that well, she did have just one passion—and that was for chocolate.

Why not buy into that wonderful franchise, Death by Chocolate, I asked? (If you love chocolate, try it. **Everything** is chocolate there, though you can get a cup of coffee if you insist.)

Another client only likes to play golf and drink fine wines. So now he organises golf and wine tours around the world.

A friend is passionate about music and has a thriving business throughout the country aimed at ensuring children learn to play the piano in the best way possible. She travelled the world seeking the best system, found it in Japan, and made that her standard.

Similarly, another friend is passionate about helping children to be the best at maths and has franchised her system throughout the country.

So what is your passion?

On the following page, write down the things you are good at and love to do.

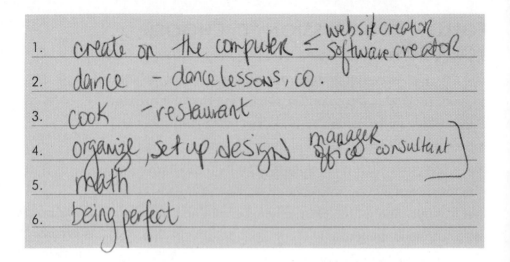

1. create on the computer ≤ website creator, software creator
2. dance - dance lessons, co.
3. cook - restaurant
4. organize, set up, design office manager, consultant
5. math
6. being perfect

Now write down businesses that match the list, businesses you could get involved in, that are already clearly understood by the immediate world around you. (I say 'the immediate world' because the richest lode of your life is right outside your front door. Just as you see far more of your friends at the bottom of the street than those across the country, you will do far more business with associates that are nearby.)

Seek a 'hole' or a refinement in the marketplace for the products or services that you are passionate about. That way you are offering something similar to what is clearly understood, but now you are adding that something extra.

Here's an example. A young man started up his own pharmacy in the busiest walkway of a large city. Some thousands of people rushed past each day, to and from their buses and trains. 'Rushed past' is the truth—his store was empty for months.

This emptiness was soon matched by his bank account, so he sadly put out 'Closing Down Sale' notices. Hundreds of people now rushed **into** his pharmacy, delighted to be buying at such good discounts!

Suddenly he was making money, hand over fist. He went on to open many more pharmacies in high traffic areas, all of them offering big, fat discounts. And yes, he is a very rich man today.

Perhaps you would like to run a restaurant? Many have tried and many have failed, but here's a story of a restaurant which could never fail. Two sisters dreamed their 'run-your-own-restaurant dream'. Their only problem was that they had very little money. But they travelled extensively in their old car, looking for a miracle. They found it in a small village: an old, run-down restaurant for sale for a song.

They scrubbed, cleaned, tidied, decorated and then did their research. They asked the local shopkeepers what food and wines and spirits the wives and mothers bought for their families—and listened carefully to the answers!

Then they invited six couples from the village to come to their restaurant, all clean and bright, to tell them what items they should put on the menu. As they suspected, the husbands liked the food they always had at home, and the wives were interested in different, exciting foods that they seldom had the opportunity to eat, at home or elsewhere.

With these six couples, the sisters defined their first menu, cooked the dishes, refined the dishes, then finally satisfied the various needs of their 12 tasters. Then came another clever touch: they named those advisers on their opening menu.

They opened to a full house. The advisers brought guests and friends, the locals came, too, because they had heard all about the new menus, and the restaurant was an instant success. It remained so, as every month another six couples were chosen to advise on the next menu—and their names too appeared on it.

'When you know what you want and want it badly enough, you'll find a way to get it.'
Jim Rohn

The fame of these wise sisters spread far and wide. Their only problem now is the waiting list of people wanting to advise!

So ask yourself how easily could you do what you have a passion for, with some thinking that is slightly outside the norm—

and therefore very successful. Remember to do something that everyone understands, but with a different little twist.

Start a hairdressing salon, for instance, that is open 24 hours a day. I know of gyms in New York that stay open 24 hours because, after all, so many people work shifts, or are night owls or early risers. Others go to gym late at night after a heavy meal, in the hope that they can shift it before it sticks!

It is your passion that drives you to a good product

Earlier we said that the three musts for a successful business are:

- Good product
- Good marketing
- Good financial management.

If you have a passion for something that the world already understands, needs and uses regularly, you are likely to have a good product. When you add an extra benefit to it (as in being a discount pharmacy, a stay-open-late hairdressing salon or gym), you have an extra benefit to talk about, which will lift you out of the crowd. Now you have a better product than your competitor, but one that is still easily understood. Your marketing then comes naturally, as you stress the benefits to your clients and prospects.

Another example: When I was with the Inter-Continental Hotel group, we analysed the performance of top-class restaurants, medium-priced, value-for-money restaurants and cheap 'n' greasy restaurants, in recession times.

The very expensive top-class restaurants suffered badly, the cheap and greasy also did badly, but the medium-priced-value-for-money restaurants did just fine in good times and bad.

Yes, being successful can be as simple as modelling success.

Here's another example: A new kind of bakery started up. It did **not** do the baking (yes, that's new). The proprietors simply invited local people to bring in their best baking, and a panel tested it for quality and taste. Those whose cakes and biscuits and breads passed the panel's scrutiny became regular suppliers to the local outlet. Once a good chocolate brownie, for instance, was accepted, nobody else could get in that category, until there was a vacancy or a drop in quality.

The costs of production were less than that of a normal bakery, and therefore the price of the products was a little lower. And the quality was high.

What is to stop you starting up a no-baking bakery, using the resources of the local people? And if you had an outlet near a school, you could tap that market, too. Value-for-money lunches made by the parents could be a great new-business idea.

So make sure that your idea of a good product is already proven by existing market response. Then add a minor and needed variation so that your product or service is still easily understood and still offers excellent value for money.

WHAT ABOUT A FRANCHISE?

Before you make your final decision to be an entrepreneur, consider buying a successful franchise. Why? Because you can then both own your own business **and** benefit from an infrastructure that doesn't exist when you are on your own. Plus, with a good franchise operation, you get good product, good marketing and good financial management.

Here are some of the advantages of buying a franchise:

- Lesser risk, providing your research shows that the franchise is a proven success or likely to be so.

- Training provided in the skills required, with the necessary technical advice.
- Access to finance through banks, which view your chances of success as being higher than when you are totally on your own.
- Advertising: the public knows the name, and the corporate advertising keeps reminding them.
- Promotions: special activities to draw in the crowds, designed at head office with a common theme and used locally.
- PR: stories and articles in main media and local media are easier to place when you are part of a bigger whole.
- Retraining: you and your staff are retrained as new products, new services, new systems come along.
- Research and development: ongoing in good franchises, and you get the benefits.
- Managerial skills at head office, lightening your load and letting you get on with being successful locally.
- Quality control: head office standards should result in fewer customer complaints.
- Specialist assistance: franchisors may provide the services of specialists in tax, labor law, market research, finances.

The Franchisee's Test

If you answer **yes** to a high number of the following questions, you are a likely candidate for being a franchisee rather than starting up a business entirely on your own. (Again my thanks to ABSA for the following questions.)

- Are you willing to run the risk of owning your own business?
- Are you prepared to put in part or all of your savings?
- Are you prepared to work long hours?
- Will your family support you in this? (One of the major

insurance companies said recently that the single most important factor in succeeding in a new business was the unwavering commitment and support of the family.)

- Can you follow directions from others?
- Can you take orders from others?
- Are you a systematic worker who can adapt to the systems, procedures and demands of a head office?
- Are you comfortable working with others?
- Do you consciously seek to help people grow?
- Are you well skilled in business and therefore easily able to master a new business?
- Do you have a passion for this franchise? If not, choose another.
- Are your assets such that you can get bank finance?

Consider carefully any 'no' answers, particularly if your partner or family do not want you to be your own boss. You may not get any support or sympathy for the long hours and hard work.

'I am a kind of paranoiac in reverse. I suspect people of plotting to make me happy.'
J. D. Salinger

The good news about franchises: Statistics are all in favour of a successful franchise continuing to be successful. It costs more up front in that your entry fee can be substantial, but you have the advantage of a ready market.

A good franchise operator only allows a franchise where there is a clearly identified market need. So when you open you have a bunch of customers, willing and wanting.

An example: McDonalds only allows another facility to open when the size of families in the local population will support the outlet.

Start out expecting to say 'no' to any franchise, or own-your-own business opportunity that you are looking at.

Ask around, visit fairs, visit franchises you would like to be part of, dream your personal dreams of owning your own business, and never, never, never make a decision in a rush.

Example of a rush to say yes:

The company that I worked with in London specialised in executive recruitment and recruitment advertising. Their owners (Saatchi & Saatchi) offered the management and staff the opportunity to buy the business.

The price put was around thirteen million pounds, most of which (obviously) had to be borrowed by the then salaried employees. The bank that was going to put up the money spent months looking at the business (a process otherwise known as due diligence), presumably checking for good product, good marketing and good financial management.

All the staff were invited to share in the buy-out, and most did. Then, half an hour before the massive borrowing was due to be signed, the bank pulled out, leaving the management with a huge bill—for the bank's time!

Retrospectively, the management should never had got into the buy-out. Why? Because the business was made up almost entirely of consultants who went home at night and came back in the morning (or not, depending on their attitude to the job).

The only real assets were some furniture and some relatively expensive computers. We later estimated that it would have cost only £250,000 to have moved the whole staff and start up in other offices close by.

So it meant that the asking price of thirteen million pounds was based almost entirely on the name. No product as such, just the name! And not that famous a name either. So do not be in a hurry to buy or start a business. Beware of snatching a bargain that may prove to be otherwise later.

FURTHER CONSIDERATIONS
Why is the business for sale?

Here are some reasons why businesses are for sale (as opposed to the reasons they may give you face to face).

1. Cash flow problems, due to the inability to finance rapidly increasing sales, and/or the inability to pay creditors (that is, suppliers who are owed money).

2. The business is based on heavy borrowings from outside sources, so that when there is a downturn in the market, or the cost of borrowing increases, profits may slide.

3. Need for substantial additional capital for various reasons, such as replacing old equipment, or bringing in new equipment to remain competitive. Or perhaps a partner is leaving and the owners cannot afford to pay out his share. This was the case with a wine farm recently. There were three partners, two active on the wine farm, the other a major investor. The third got in trouble elsewhere, so the flourishing wine farm had to be sold.

4. Price cutting by competitors is forcing them out of business. Major players in an industry segment will let little people in, just so long as they don't affect their market share to any great degree.

   But when the little guy gets noticeably bigger, the big guys drop their prices lower and lower and lower. The little guy matches them as long as he can, then goes bust.

   It is not by accident that the biggest names in most industry sectors were the first into the market. They stay on top by waging price wars on companies that get in their way.

5. Performance has peaked and the owner wants to sell on a high, particularly if competitors are coming in with a

'Only Irish coffee provides in a single glass all four essential food groups: alcohol, caffeine, sugar and fat.'
Alex Levine

newer, better product. (Well, wouldn't you?)

6. Lack of qualified management, or the inability to attract them to the business. Or it may be a family business with no one in the wings to take over, or perhaps a key staff member has left and a suitable replacement has not been found.

    If, in your research, you find a problem that you can fix, then consider buying the business, but only at a price that reflects the cost of solving the problem.

Next, beware the contract

Sign nothing in haste. Have everything checked thoroughly by a good lawyer and accountant before you sign. Note that a contract is only a series of words, all of which can be changed with the other party's approval, before you sign.

Nothing is cast in stone until signed, and even then it can be challenged, but at a price, and in the end only the lawyers will win.

If you don't have the guts to negotiate, to argue for a better deal, to challenge the contract for good reasons and stick to your guns, you should not, **repeat not,** be going into business on your own.

Yes, do follow your passion, but with care.

The truth of being a start-up entrepreneur is this:

1. The business takes at least twice as long to get up and running as you expect or plan.
2. It costs at least twice as much as you ever thought it would to promote, hire, buy equipment, desks, etc., etc. (just like your personal/family budget).
3. And you will earn about half the profit you expect (just as your family savings are far less than you expect).

If your business plan still looks viable matched up against this endlessly proven wisdom, then you may well succeed.

Remember, it is far easier to get into something than it is to get out of it. Consider marriage v. divorce, buying a house v. selling it, making babies v. being a parent. The same goes for buying a business v. running it or on-selling it. Make haste slowly.

Next, reflect on what you are giving up when you leave corporate life! Many soon-to-be entrepreneurs have little idea of what their real salary and benefits are. It is usual for a company to have to multiply the employee's salary by at least three times to reach the real cost of having that person on the payroll.

After salary, additional costs include car and its many expenses, medical insurance, pension and retirement provision, life and disability insurance, holidays and expense accounts.

'Organised crime takes in over forty billion dollars a year and spends very little on office supplies.'
Woody Allen

Plus of course office space, phone bills, support staff, stationery, postage, wear and tear on equipment, share of heating, lighting, and an amazing sum on coffee, tea and biscuits!

Then, too, you will be in a different tax bracket, and although you will have more deductions, you will have to pay an accountant to do your books—which could well eat up the difference.

I have talked with many new entrepreneurs who cannot operate a computer, type a letter, send a fax, do a budget or make a sales call by phone or face-to-face, let alone create or find a file. Corporate life cares for us too well at times! So their first cost is a personal assistant to do all the things they took for granted. Up go the expenses again.

Moreover, many executives have never had to sell

themselves. They have worked in cash-cow industries where the business just fell through the door, and now, as an entrepreneur, they can't get used to the idea that the phone doesn't ring with the orders.

Again they have to hire salespeople up front to do what they should be doing until the business is on its feet. That is another heavy start-up cost.

There are many more challenges on the way, such as loss of good staff. You have trained them well, given time, energy and money to making them great—and they get head-hunted by the opposition for more money, better benefits.

Research shows that if you match or better the new offer, and the person stays, they will be gone within 18 months anyway. Why? It seems that the sense of trust is broken after that first resignation letter, and the relationship goes sour.

Rewarding excellence early on is a way of holding good people, people your new business needs.

Further concerns that may be awaiting you: On the money side, you may find yourself in a highly price-competitive market, so your profit margins are low and you have to work harder and harder just to stand still. The situation can be made worse by slow-paying debtors, increased expenses due to higher bank overdraft rates, higher prices of materials through currency fluctuations or just bad old inflation.

'The government which robs Peter to pay Paul can always rely on the support of Paul.'
George Bernard Shaw (1856–1950)

New competitors may offer similar goods or services at lower prices, the demand for your product or service may shift (look at the mad cow disease disaster) or you may grow rapidly and find that costs outstrip income.

Creditors may press you just when you least need it, and the unions may take some disastrous action.

Then there is entrepreneurial burn out: when you are

doing too many jobs because you can't afford the staff, and one day your body just gives up. Where you did not have time for lunch, you are now sick in bed with 'flu.

An estimate from America recently: the cost of a face-to-face sales call was US$2,600—whether or not you got the business. You can see why you need far more money than you might expect since few sales are made on the first call, and each call thereafter will still cost US$2,600. Investments like these need big back-up.

So remember, when you leave corporate life to run your own business, you will need more money, not less, and much of it will go into that seemingly bottomless pit called your dream.

'At the end of the day you should play back the tapes of your performance. The results will either applaud you or prod you.'
Jim Rohn

How long will it take to be successful?

If you are starting up a new business (i.e., not a franchise), the first two years are usually unremitting hard work; it is usually only in the third year that you begin to think you have a business with some money left over for you.

After about the fourth or fifth year of long hours, hard work, and constant re-investment of your hard-won profits, you will feel that you are getting there.

Opening up additional offices or outlets is somewhat easier now, as you have all that the experience of the past years has taught you and can use it wisely.

After ten years or so, you may well have learned enough to be able to say that you truly have a business, and you know how you did it. In other words, you now feel you can repeat your successes.

A quicker route to success is, of course, to take advice from someone who truly knows what he or she is doing, and follow it.

Here's a recent example: In the heart of a European community already well served with pastry shops, a young woman and her partner opened yet another such shop. It was overwhelmingly successful from the first month.

Why? Because they took advice from a top hotelier who understood the market, what the people would buy, what the shop should look like, what the marketing should be. The result is history. They got the 'three threes' of success together: good product, good marketing and good financial management.

Remember, a good product is one that the market wants and will pay for at that time, but be sure to take note of changing trends and be there to meet them.

Good marketing and selling is what this book is all about. But what constitutes good financial management? To me it is as Charles Dickens described it:

'Income one pound, outgoings one pound and a penny: result—unhappiness.

Income one pound, outgoings nineteen shillings and eleven pence: result—happiness.'

A speaker on air the other day said that many entrepreneurs confuse **cash flow with income,** not realising, or wanting to realise, that **expenses have to come out of income before you have cash flow.** So they spend what comes in, fail to pay their bills, and the result is unhappiness for all concerned, workers and creditors alike.

If being in your own business is your passion, then go for it.

'It is better to know some of the questions than all of the answers.'
James Thurber
(1894–1961)

Take good advice from people who are experienced and successful in the kind of business you plan to start, and act on it. Be sure to understand all the aspects of being in business so that you have a good product, promoted well through good marketing and sales, and good financial management.

Cheques should be signed by yourself and one other (never by an employee or associate on their own), and you must know on a **daily basis** what your true cash flow situation is, that is, income less costs. Remember, savings must be put aside for growing your business, and for a 'tough times' fund.

In all the years I have been travelling and consulting, I have found that the most common and destructive fraud inside companies is (naturally) to do with money directly.

Accountants move money into other (personal) accounts; staff put blank cheques in the middle of the bunch (later filling in their own names) which you unknowingly sign as you whizz through the pile; they create fake invoices and receipts for petty cash, and so it goes.

Fraud may go undetected for years, as in this example: One of the great hotel chains had a star property that for years had not been making as much money as it should, but they could not understand why.

Then one day their liquor supplier rang up and asked if it were possible that the hotel could be using over 20 cases of **Moet et Chandon** a month. 'No way,' came the astonished answer.

A new regional sales manager had been appointed at the liquor supplier, and he had been checking back over the past few years. He had noticed that a large liquor store nearby had stopped ordering **Moet et Chandon** some three years back—about the same time this fine hotel had started ordering it, 20 cases at a time.

White collar crime and computer crime is rampant and many, many people have said to me that they lost everything through trusting, rather than checking. Don't let it happen to you as an entrepreneur.

If the advantages of being a franchise holder appear more

'Men and nations behave wisely once they have exhausted all the other alternatives.'
Abba Eban

to your liking, then buy a franchise. Good financial management is built into a good franchise, so the chances of fraud going undetected for long are a little less.

The choice is yours . . . Good luck!

KEY POINTS TO REMEMBER:

- Make haste slowly; it is easier to get into something than it is to get out of it.
- The longer you spend thinking about a problem, the quicker the solution. Many people rush into things and then spend a lifetime fixing the result.
- Follow your passion, but only if it is easily understood. Life is too short and there is too little money to create a new understanding in our already over-stressed brains.
- Once you have found your passion, try to add a little extra to your product or service, so that the buying populace quickly sees and understands the benefit.

'Nobody has ever bet enough on a winning horse.'
Overheard at a track by Richard Sasuly

※ ※ ※

The next part of this book will tell you how to grow your business (and this knowledge is just as valuable whether you are starting up on your own, buying a franchise, or still working in a corporation).

Read on to learn from my experience over more than two decades of working and travelling and learning with some of the biggest and some of the smallest companies in the world.

From now on you will be deliberately successful. Remember being excellent is NOT optional. You will know which of the many techniques make the difference, and you will succeed because of that knowledge—but only if you actively use that information.

As someone said to me recently, it is funny how 'do-it-yourself' books work better when you do it yourself.

GROWTH SKILL 1

STAY IN TOUCH WITHIN 90 DAYS

Keep in touch with your prospect **and** client base regularly and relentlessly within 90 days. Less than 90 days is fine, but never let more than 90 days go by without contact—which is approximately 60 working days.

Proven by Saatchi and Saatchi's London advertising agency over twenty years and (accidently) by me during my time with the Inter-Continental Hotel Group in Australia, this is the missing link in most people's business development process. It was certainly missing in mine for far too many years.

I well remember those crazy conversations where we asked the 'gurus' how often we should stay in touch and they answered, 'As often as is necessary'. Now intensive research has shown us that 90 days is how often.

'I never forget a face, but in your case I will gladly make an exception.'
Groucho Marx (1895–1997)

WORLD ROUND-UP OF PROOF

In London: What Saatchi & Saatchi found was that the people they had been contacting by phone and face to face had a clear enough memory of the previous call and conversation for up to 90 days. After that, it was as though the mind had cleared itself of all memory.

In Sydney: LJ Hooker Real Estate's general manager had a similar experience. He and I had met, then our next appointment was moved and re-booked for the first week of the fourth month following. The first thing he said was that he was going to put the whole of LJ Hooker on the 90-day cycle.

When I queried why, he said that for 90 days I had been clear in his mind—almost as though I were in the room with him when he thought of me—but on the first day of the fourth month, I had shrunk to the size of a jelly bean!

In Hong Kong: At Saatchi & Saatchi's Hong Kong agency, working for our client Procter and Gamble, we stayed in touch with 100,000 mothers every three months, advising them that their babies were growing slowly and steadily and it was time to move up to the next size of Pampers. We enclosed a 'price-off' voucher to make the next purchase very affordable.

Our research had showed that mothers blamed the Pampers product when the baby grew too big for its previous size to be effective. Because of this, around 50 per cent of mothers in other countries had stopped buying disposable diapers. We did not want that to happen in Hong Kong!

Through this quarterly educational program, we grew our market share from 13 per cent to 42 per cent and each point was worth US$1 million over the life cycle of the product.

In Melbourne: Representing the Inter-Continental Hotel Group worldwide (some 60 hotels), I called on the major players in the travel industry **every day.** (Yes, that is taking the 90-day or less cycle to an extreme!) Through reward, recognition and an almost perfect reservations system, we grew the business from 200 room nights per month to 2001.

'The average person thinks he isn't.'
Father Larry Lorenzo

Then New York Head Office wanted the training program on how we did it, so I was locked away for several months writing, designing, refining and getting it ready. For three months those room nights stayed at their highest point. Then in the first week of the fourth month, the bookings crashed.

The travel industry gave all the business—and more—to the Hilton Hotel group, who came through at that time with a special promotion. The Hilton Group must have been amazed at the results.

When I met David Miln at Saatchi & Saatchi in London and he said that they had found the 90-day cycle was the maximum time for staying in touch, I said, 'I have that graph'. Then I told him the whole wonderful and sad story of the Inter-Continental Hotel bookings and their rise and fall.

We shook hands on the truth of the 90-day cycle and agreed that when people have developed trust and belief in you and your product, and then you walk away, you can lose all that you have gained, and more.

Once you get on the 90-day cycle, stay with it or you will have wasted all your previous time, energy and money.

More in London: At Saatchi's executive recruitment company, I used the 90-day cycle for having open days and top-name speakers, like Charles Handy and Sir John Harvey Jones, to attract prospects into the offices of MSL, where they would meet and get to know the staff. With 400 major companies as our prospects, we gained many of them within two years.

New York: My client, a small start-up company called IMCOR: the Interim Management Corporation, had been choking the life out of too few friends. We identified 8000 more prospects through the use of the commonality survey (more about that soon) across America, and contacted them by mail and follow-up phone call every three months.

By the fifth cycle of mailing and phone calls, IMCOR were getting around 60 per cent acceptance to appointments to discuss the use of their very senior interim/temporary management executives. This is the normal success rate with the regular, relentless follow-up within 90 days.

Make your new-business program an integral part of your daily operations, and you can choose clients you want to work

'I do not want people to be agreeable, as it saves me the trouble of liking them.'
Jane Austen
(1775–1817)

with as the opportunities arrive from your contact process, spread over 60 working days (or less if you wish).

Even if your customers and prospects will probably not buy again for a few years (for example, another car), you still have to keep in touch once every three months so that you'll be in the running when they are ready to purchase again.

In South Africa a client commented that he had been buying a new BMW every year for seven years and had never had a contact of any sort from the agents he had used in that time.

He had moved from agent to agent as a test, waiting to see which one would contact him. (I am pleased to say that he is now completely spoilt by contacts, not necessarily because I wrote about it in my previous book.)

Both clients and prospects must be contacted within the three-month period. Leave your clients in your prospecting system. Do not shift them into a separate 'done-and-forgotten' file. Remember that they are somebody else's prospects. Remember, too, that you get more business from people who are already buying from you, so your clients are still prospects in that sense also.

Make this Saatchi & Saatchi 90-day system work for you. Three is the magic number. Have you been contacting your clients and prospects within three months or less, or only when you have time? Have they learned to trust you because you always stay in contact, regularly and in a professional manner? Or are you an infrequent caller because you are too busy?

Of course, no one is ever there when you phone, so send a greeting card, a relevant PR piece or brochure and a note saying that you will be in touch again within three (or two or one) months. And do it! Be sure to enclose your business card every time. (Your last one was probably mislaid.)

'It is the first time I have bought a business book and got back over $250,000.'
Mike Johr

KEY POINTS TO REMEMBER

- Build relationships regularly and relentlessly, creatively and caringly. Make regular contact within 90 days. You can wait less than 90 days if you wish, but never more than ninety days, otherwise you lose more than you gain.
- Divide your total prospects by the 60 working days in three months and see, hear and feel how easily you can incorporate contacting them into your daily business life.
- Keep moving—simply send a note, a greeting card, whatever, if you do not reach your prospects or clients by phone, and keep on regularly and relentlessly. One day you will get through to those well-chosen likely buyers and they will remember you from your regular communications. Always enclose your business card.

> 'It took me twenty years of studied self restraint, aided by the natural decay of my faculties, to make myself dull enough to be accepted as a serious person by the British public.'
> **George Bernard Shaw (1856–1950)**

   When I ring my clients around the world and ask them, 'Of all the things we said and did together, what made the difference?' they reply as if with one voice, 'Not feeling guilty until 91 days.'

- If you want to kick-start your business super-fast, stay in touch every week, every fortnight, every month, or every two months.
- If you have more time, use the full three-month cycle. Why? Because prospects and clients can feel threatened if you contact too often; 90 days seems the perfect time scale for feeling nurtured.
- Keep your clients in your prospect base, as you will always get more business from people who are already happy dealing with you.

■ ■ ■

Next step: the hunters and the farmers, and how both are needed in building and maintaining a successful business.

GROWTH SKILL 2

TO GROW YOUR BUSINESS YOU NEED BOTH HUNTERS AND FARMERS

'Civilisation exists by geological consent, subject to changes without notice.'
Will Durant (1885–1981)

Here are some questions to help you decide whether you are a hunter or a farmer:

ARE YOU A HUNTER?

- Are you excited and thrilled by the chase?
- Is winning everything?
- Is each day an adventure?
- Do you follow up well?
- Do you live on the edge and love it?
- Do you enjoy being by yourself?
- Do you also enjoy being with people?
- Do you have so many things to do that you barely have time to sleep?
- Does your brain buzz with new ideas, new ways of doing things?

If so, in all probability, you're a hunter.

ARE YOU A FARMER?

- Do you prefer to build relationships rather than say 'hi' and run?
- Are you more comfortable in known surroundings than coping with new countries, new languages, new foods?

- Do you prefer an organised day to always having to rush to another appointment?
- Are you quite shy of new people and prefer to be with those you know?
- Do you like to take time to understand the other person's needs and enjoy filling those needs?
- Do you feel strongly about doing your work well and properly?
- Do you hate to be rushed into doing a job?

If all this is true of you, it seems likely you will flourish in the farming role.

When the business grows to the point of sharing the roles, if you prefer hunting, keep the hunting/prospecting role for yourself. If you'd rather be back at the ranch checking the finances, supervising the staff, meeting ongoing client needs, then stay in that farming role.

THE RIGHT PEOPLE FOR THE RIGHT JOB

Here's a personality profile analysis to help you choose the right person for the right job. You will note that the first two columns are labelled 'Higher energy people' and the last two, 'Lower energy people'. High energy people need to be out and about (hunting) and lower energy people like to be back inside, caring for the business.

From left to right, the first column describes 'Inspirers', those suited primarily to head up a large organisation. They are highly charismatic people, with no liking for detail, so they need a large support system at all times. They make quick decisions relative to whether or not they are entertained and amused by the person selling to them. They are very casual with company money and never get receipts, so cannot explain or account for their large advances. They are

'Good judgement comes from experience and experience comes from bad judgement.'
Barry LePatner

always at loggerheads with the accountant in the firm.

The second column, 'Aspirers', are ideal in the sales role or for starting up a new business. They are tenacious and will ensure that things happen. They make quick decisions based on a few facts, and fix things up afterwards, if necessary. They are highly independent and resent being told, though will be advised respectfully. These two personality styles are high energy and make good hunters.

The next personality, the 'Enquirer', is the accountant type who wants more and more detail and who is ideal in that job, but is a low level decision-maker, since he or she needs so much detail in order to get near to a conclusion. Suspicious by nature, Enquirers will only ever give small pieces of the business to any one supplier, in order not to be vulnerable at any time.

The 'Admirers' are best in human resources roles and are characterised by the need to chat for 20 minutes before getting down to business. They make slow decisions, based on whether it will benefit the **people** of the organisation. These two styles are low energy, and quite contented in the farmer role.

Hire according to these profiles, and your success ratio will soar.

KEY POINTS TO REMEMBER:

- If the wrong person gets into either role, the hunting will be ineffective and prospects who do become clients will be left unattended.
- For every strength we have, we may well have a matching weakness. No one is perfect, so build on the strengths, help your staff overcome their weaknesses.

■ ■ ■

PERSONALITY PROFILE—STRENGTHS

Note to user: Respond as you are *at work*; we often behave quite differently at home. Please mark off one word on each line **across** that you feel most aptly describes you at work. Don't think too long, just do it as quickly and as honestly as you can. Your highest score is your dominant style.

Higher energy people		Lower energy people	
1. Animated	Persuasive	Planner	Adaptable
2. Refreshing	Sure	Orderly	Peaceful
3. Cheerful	Daring	Idealistic	Submissive
4. Demonstrative	Adventurous	Perfectionist	Considerate
5. Bouncy	Independent	Self-sacrificing	Respectful
6. Playful	Decisive	Controlled	Satisfied
7. Spontaneous	Tenacious	Sensitive	Patient
8. Delightful	Chieftain	Faithful	Shy
9. Sociable	Bold	Musical	Obliging
10. Outspoken	Competitive	Loyal	Friendly
11. Funny	Self-reliant	Analytical	Diplomatic
12. Talkative	Positive	Persistent	Consistent
13. Convincing	Mover	Reserved	Inoffensive
14. Spirited	Leader	Scheduled	Dry humour
15. Promoter	Productive	Cultured	Mediator
16. Inspiring	Strong-willed	Mapmaker	Tolerant
17. Easy mixer	Resourceful	Balanced	Listener
18. Cute	Optimistic	Detailed	Contented
19. Popular	Forceful	Thoughtful	Permissive
20. Lively	Confident	Deep	Well-behaved

**

Total ....

Inspirer	Aspirer	Enquirer	Admirer
Corporate Head/Visionary	Entrepreneur	Accountant	Human Resources

**Add down the columns and write in totals above.

You may want to get applicants to tick their weaknesses too.

PERSONALITY PROFILE—WEAKNESSES

Higher energy people		Lower energy people	
1. Brassy	Impatient	Reluctant	Fussy
2. Undisciplined	Unpopular	Plain ordinary	Too sensitive
3. Naive	Headstrong	Worrier	Doubtful
4. Inconsistent	Easily angered	Low energies	Loner
5. Messy	Bossy	Sluggish	Insecure
6. Haphazard	Unsympathetic	Revengeful	Pessimistic
7. Disorganised	Resentful	Compromising	Negative
8. Forgetful	Tactless	Fearful	Withdrawn
9. Unpredictable	Stubborn	Uninvolved	Moody
10. Argumentative	Lordly	Suspicious	Selfish
11. Show-off	Restless	Introvert	Critical
12. Interruptive	Proud	Indecisive	Hard to please
13. Permissive	Edgy/nervy	Timid	Slow to respond
14. Wants credit	Workaholic	Mumbles	Unaffectionate
15. Talkative	Domineering	Lazy	Alienated
16. Loud	Intolerant	Blank	Indifferent
17. Scatterbrain	Short-tempered	Unforgiving	Sceptical
18. Rash	Crafty	Hesitant	Bashful
19. Changeable	Manipulative	Nonchalant	Unenthusiastic
20. Resistant	Frank	Depressed	Repetitious
**			

Total ....

Inspirer	Aspirer	Enquirer	Admirer
Visionary/	Entrepreneur	Accountant	Human
Head of			Resources
Large Corpn			

**Add down the columns and write in totals above.

The next growth skill will tell you how to identify your best prospects, simply and effectively.

GROWTH SKILL 3
BUILD RELATIONSHIPS WITH WELL-CHOSEN PROSPECTS DEFINED THROUGH THE COMMONALITY SURVEY

Instead of choking the life out of too few prospects, build relationships with many.

Whenever I am speaking or training or consulting, I ask the group to put up their hands if they have ever had a second contact from a salesperson to whom they first said, 'No,' quite firmly.

In a room of about one hundred people, I might get 10 hands up. Then I ask them to keep their hands up if they have ever had a third contact from that same salesperson and, almost without exception, those few hands go down.

It seems that all over the world most salespeople make one contact and, if refused, keep moving to the next and the next and the next prospect. Yet we know from the considerable amount of client money spent across the world, **that it is by the fifth contact to the same prospect that you get up to 60 per cent acceptance** to a meeting or to the purchase of your product or service.

Example: Proctor & Gamble's Pampers product had 13 per cent market share in Hong Kong. Determined to be number one, we at Saatchi & Saatchi Advertising in Hong Kong went on a massive campaign to gather in the names and addresses of mothers and babies, through highly successful cash-back

'When all is said and done, more is said than done.'
Unknown.

sales promotion activities. To get the cash back, mothers had to write in with full names and address details as well as baby's birth date and sex.

Using this information we wrote to the mothers on a quarterly basis, telling them of their baby's growth and what to expect at these various stages. We also sent out discount vouchers when it was time to buy the next size up, so that the diaper always performed well.

Within 14 months (that is, into the fifth cycle of three-monthly contacts to the same ever-growing list of mothers) Pampers had moved into the number one position with 49 per cent market share. We would have gone to 55 per cent market share, but the product got hijacked out of Japan, where it was manufactured and black-marketed in Taiwan.

That was a great compliment to our work, but lost us quite a few percentage points, while we were persuading the pirates to let us have our product in Hong Kong.

'The school of hard knocks is an accelerated curriculum.'
Menander
(342–292 B.C.)

Does this re-contacting of a well-chosen band of prospects work for smaller start-up companies? Yes it does!

Here is a New York example: A new start-up company called IMCOR (short for the Interim Management Corporation) had been choking the life out of too few prospects (their associates from their previous corporate positions).

They sought 21st-century marketing skills, and I was chosen out of London. When we met, I asked them what their current clients had in common. From their answers (small to medium-sized companies in specific industries), I was then able to find them a further 8000 likely prospects across America.

Then I designed a strong new corporate identity in blue and white and gold, and we mailed those 8000 companies across three months, with a follow-up call to each the week following (to allow time for the mail to arrive and be read).

By the fifth cycle they were getting up to 60 per cent acceptance to meeting or using the service—which consisted of very senior executives being leased out on temporary assignments.

THERE ARE MANY WAYS OF STAYING IN TOUCH

Throughout my working life I have been struck by how similar business is to our personal lives. You can wreck it or build it depending on your attitude and behaviour. The nudging process of business development is much the same as the way we look after our relationships with the people we care about.

'The art of living is more like wrestling than dancing.'
Marcus Aurelius (121–80 B.C.)

Unbidden, we will think of them and invite them for lunch, or take an extra cup of coffee in to talk over a problem. We will send a memo or a fax as an update on something of importance to them.

We might send them a magazine cutting. Meet them at an airport. Buy them a book we found of value. Send a postcard. Remember their birthday. Invite them to our Christmas, New Year or birthday party. Without quite knowing how, we have stayed in touch because it is easy, pleasant and rewarding.

You need do no more in your nudging of prospects. It is not hard to have lunch with someone you have grown to like. It is nice to come by for coffee, having first checked to see if it suits. You can pass on an opinion about a movie they have expressed an interest in.

Sharing magazine articles is a very kind gesture in an overloaded world, as are newspaper clippings from editions outside the usual. For instance I have just faxed overseas a report on an excellent wine which I think my hotel client would like to add to his wine list.

Postcards from abroad please the whole office, especially if you're having a terrible time in a typhoon.

Remembering birthdays is a knockout and it is even more fun to research the foundation date of the company and send a birthday cake. The effect is highly impressive. I once won a conference and dinner booking at an Inter-Continental hotel for many hundreds of people by doing just that a year in advance of a company's 100-year anniversary.

I sent a cake and a letter saying: 'On this day next year you will be celebrating your 100th anniversary, and we would be delighted to be the venue of choice.'

The bonus was that the company had no idea until then that it was their centenary! So they were delighted to have a year up their sleeves to plan for it. And yes, we got the booking on the spot! Nudging a wide band of well-chosen prospects is fun. It's creative, it's rewarding and it makes a lot of people happy, including you.

So how wide can this band of well-chosen prospects be? As you read earlier, in Hong Kong we had 100,000 names on our data base. That regular, relentless, without-fail contacting every three months increased our market share from 13 per cent to 42 per cent—and each point was worth US$1,000,000, over the life usage of the product. That's US$29,000,00 just by staying in touch with the same base, within three months, over and over.

At Thomas Cook's we had over 60,000 leisure travellers 'captured' by 20 or more parameters. In London we had 400 companies that I was pursuing. In New York it was 8,000 across America. It is amazing what you can do with computer generated mailings and follow-up phone calls.

My favourite creative ice breaker is one I learned in a Tony Robbins' seminar: send in a breakfast basket of croissant, orange juice, marmalade, butter and a small knife, with a note saying, 'My ideas are as fresh and as classical as the breakfast I send you.' I sign the note 'W'.

Later that day, I sent in my book, saying, 'My ideas are as fresh and as classical as the breakfast I sent you today. I will call you for an appointment. Enjoy!' And I signed the greeting card and the book in full. Yes, I do get an appointment every time.

I was talking a few days ago with a salesperson who had been in that 'contact once, get a refusal and move on' cycle. She had spent two years skimming over the top of people's needs, never once going back to consolidate. She and millions of other people involved in sales. Why, I know not.

Recently I rang, faxed and wrote to a prospect. He rang me back and said crossly, 'Why are you contacting me endlessly?' And I replied, 'To prove that the 90-day cycle works.' He laughed and said, 'You're right, come on in.'

My favourite story is about a New York friend, Barbara Rogers. She rang me and asked if I had told Jim Johnson to call her. I said, 'No, who is Jim Johnson?'

'Well,' she said, 'He rang me and said, oh so nicely, that he was sure I was happy with my current accountant but if not, he would like to take that role. I replied that I was well looked after and he then said, "Thank you, Mrs Rogers, and if I may, I will call you back on Monday in four weeks time at 3 p.m., just to check."'

And he did, on the dot. And he got the job. Why? Because as Barbara said, he was the only person who had ever called her twice, let alone on the dot of the day and time stated. She said, 'If he runs his business as well as this, imagine what he could do for mine.'

Simple, yes? Effective, yes? So why not do it!

'Never forget that the most powerful force on earth is love.'
Nelson Rockefeller (1908–1979) to Henry Kissinger

DEFINE YOUR PROSPECT BASE USING THE COMMONALITY SURVEY

Many a time I struggled with the question of how to find likely new prospects in a vast city or community. Then one day I realised that I and my best friends had a lot in common, so decided therefore that the clue to getting new prospects for clients was to find out what their best clients had in common and look for more of those.

Simple—and it proved to be highly effective. Your best prospects should look like your existing best clients (and the best clients of your competition). In researching for prospective buyers, look for common threads to create your wide band of well-chosen prospects.

Ask yourself:

- What is it about your current clients that you like, in terms of their personalities and how they deal with you? Where are they geographically?
- What industries are they in?
- How many clients are male?
- How many are female?
- How many are children?
- How many are not of local origin?
- What size company are they, based on amount of revenue generated, staff size and ranking in the top one hundred?
- What are they buying from you now?
- What do they think of your product?
- Which of them have you retained easily as repeat business, and why?
- Which of them are the most profitable?

'These things pay off—good taste, a high standard of ethics, an attitude of public responsibility and low pressure.'
Leo Burnett

Talk to them and find out why they use you. Doing so may enlarge your view of what your new-business marketplace can be. Get the big picture first. Then ask about groups: minorities, men, women, children, families, older people.

It can also help you to find that single-minded proposition and that key phrase to describe your product—an invaluable shorthand way for you to present yourself to the world. (See the Growth Skill 4: 'The Single-Minded Proposition'.)

Here's a reason to ask yourself which of your existing clients are most profitable, why they are profitable and how you can use this information to define similar prospects.

Example: A jeweller researched who exactly was contributing to his bottom line. He found that non-whites buying gold gave him 32 per cent of his profit. With this information he re-allocated his media spending and lifted that market to 50 per cent of his profit.

And what clients have you lost and why? This is an issue that you will want to face squarely and examine carefully. It is of critical interest to the well-being and future growth of your business. It's rare for people to hear what they don't want to hear. Have courage. Ask, listen and learn.

While all of these issues are significant, greater weight might be given to geographical location and the personalities you most enjoy being with.

People tend to do more business with people they can reach easily and whom they like. Moreover, it is likely that there are excellent prospects within your own business district with whom you have never been in touch.

It is interesting that entrepreneurs seeking new business will often travel forty blocks, drive kilometres, jump on a plane, cross rivers and mountains, but will seldom work in their immediate locality, let alone their own office building. All they usually come back with from these trips is huge expense accounts.

'Mistakes are all there waiting to be made.'
Savielly Grigorievitch Tartakover (1887–1956)

The prospects who are physically nearest can be the richest mine of your life, because you will spend less and get a higher response from them. Find local prospects, contact them until they are ready to become clients and keep them. Remember, it is critical to have a high volume of prospects for success to follow.

'Victory goes to the player who makes the next-to-last mistake.'
Savielly Grigorievitch Tartakover (1887–1956)

The ultimate issue in your business building is the people you deal with. As much as they want quality service (and good prices and being rescued from laziness and fear), you want quality communications, respect, integrity and fair dealing. Until you get that you will not be happy.

This is why the broad band of prospects is so important: it gives you space to find the right clients. No longer are you waiting for the phone to ring; you are pursuing the right prospects, regularly and relentlessly, every 90 days or less . . . You are being proactive, not reactive.

Remember, business development is just like your personal life. You keep in touch with your friends, take an interest in their activities, help where you can with advice or actions, send cards, remember special occasions with gifts, do nice things when you can.

Similarly, you know exactly how to lose a relationship. Forget to ring, turn up late, promise but don't deliver, be abrupt when you should be patient, expect more than you are prepared to give.

All of this goes on in business and it is easier to lose a client or prospect than it is a long-term friend, who is rather more inclined to forgive and forget.

The exciting next step is to look beyond what is common into creatively relevant possibilities. For instance, Procter & Gamble noticed that some elderly people became incontinent, and created an adult product for that market.

Then in Hong Kong they found that Chinese babies were left in diapers longer than their European counterparts, so they developed an extra-large diaper for that market.

Coca-Cola foresaw the move to less sugar and more healthy living, but they launched their Diet Coke quietly until proven. Now it is promoted with great vigour. But when Coca-Cola decided to radically change their **core** product, the world rebelled, requiring them to backtrack and have Classic Coke as well as the new Coke.

See how your existing products can be modified to meet a market need, rather than create totally new products for which you have no known reputation—and which will cost a great deal of money to promote to a level of profitable acceptance.

In essence it is a matter of keeping core products as the bread and butter of a corporation while identifying and meeting changing consumer needs.

If there is a market for a modified product, you must of course analyse how your core business would be affected by this product or service variation, for better or for worse. Then make your decision accordingly.

'Either I've been missing something or nothing has been going on.'
Karen Elizabeth Gordon

Here is a sample commonality survey to help you think about your current clients in terms of what clues they can give you for choosing new clients. The survey can be adapted for past/lost clients.

Note: This survey is deceptively simple and very effective. Try it and see for yourself.

Use what you have seen in these analyses to find more of the clients you want. Find those that are most like the companies you now prefer working with.

CURRENT CLIENT COMMONALITY SURVEY

Date. _____

Name of client. _____

Distance from your office. _____

National, yes/no. _____

Multinational, yes/no. _____

Subsidiary of: _____

Names of company people you relate to and what it is that you like and dislike about each of them.

Name: _____

Like. _____

Dislike. _____

Name: _____

Like. _____

Dislike. _____

Name: _____

Like. _____

Dislike. _____

What does the client think of :

    (a)   your company's performance

_____

_____

_____

    (b)   your relationships with their people?

_____

_____

_____

Their industry sector. _____

Their product or service. _____

Size of company by revenue: Small, Medium, Large. _____

Size up/down from previous years? (explain).

_____

_____

_____

_____

CURRENT CLIENT COMMONALITY SURVEY

Staff numbers now. Growing/declining? (explain).

_____

_____

_____

Expenditure now with your company. _____

Growing or declining in expenditure? (explain).

_____

_____

_____

Client is/is not profitable? (explain).

_____

_____

_____

How do you see the next two, three, five years with this client? Will they grow with you, fade away, remain about the same? (explain).

_____

_____

_____

_____

Explain why/how the client should be: _____

Kept. _____

Replaced. _____

Revitalised. _____

If you owned the client company, what changes would you make?

_____

_____

_____

If there were an exact clone of this company, would you want to work with them? (explain).

_____

_____

_____

_____

MARKET RESEARCH

You might wish to initiate market research about a particular product or about your company's standing with consumers as measured against similar companies.

Market research can provide clues to the future. Following are some of the questions you might wish to ask in focus groups with your own customers or clients and those of similar companies.

Focus groups are used to find out what customers like and dislike and why they buy this product instead of that, as well as other issues such as quality of customer/client service, staff attitudes, product knowledge.

The groups usually meet for two hours and provide considerable insight for future action, such as extended market research surveys and enhanced prospect lists.

Questions could include:

'Let others praise ancient times; I am glad I was born in these.'
Ovid
(43 B.C.–A.D. 18)

- What type of organisations are producing similar products/services to yours?
- What are their clients' expectations and perceptions of these products and services?
- Are there regional purchasing variations? If so, what are they? And what causes them?
- What do your clients think of you as opposed to your competition?
- What do your clients see themselves needing in the future?
- Would your clients buy again? If not, why? If yes, why? And over what period of time?
- And most of all, why are people not buying from you when you have a product or service that would suit them well?

The answers to these and other questions will allow you to move your business forward from a position of knowledge. You can use the findings to help you decide many issues, among them:

- Your overall business plan and marketing strategy.
- The products and services that should be continued, discontinued, developed or enhanced.
- Likely areas for new-client development, taking local variations into account. For instance, in the colder countries, people readily go on winter holidays because they already have warm clothes in their wardrobe. In the warmer zones they prefer to go on tropical island holidays or cruises, because they live in a sun-filled, warm climate and dress accordingly. If you were providing travel, you would promote different holidays in different regions, thereby getting more value for your advertising and promotional dollar.
- The selling cycle: is it the same all year, or seasonal?
- The research, advertising, sales promotion, events, database/ direct marketing, telemarketing, training, merchandising activities, staff or outside consultancies required to 'make it all happen'.
- The public relations, corporate communication positioning activities and the staff/consultancies needed.

The results of your market research will likely increase the quality of your business and marketing plans, their implementation and thereby the flow of qualified leads to salespeople. This research will also ultimately provide customers with products and services they require.

Consider doing research on a daily basis to keep you up to date with what your clients, customers (and prospects) are

'Get your facts first, then you can distort them as you please.'
**Mark Twain
(1835–1910)**

experiencing, so that rapid action can effectively stop any problems before they set in.

This daily research can be captured by printing a number of cards with your vision statement on them and the simple question, 'Did your visit match our vision?' Ask also for their name and phone number and ring those who answered, both yes and no. It is good to get the good news to prepare you for the bad!

MAKE RESEARCH WORK FOR YOU EVERY DAY

Plan to have market research every day. If you are a retailer it can be very simple. Design an easy-to-answer, short questionnaire that your customers can fill in at reception or while they are waiting for their credit card to be approved or for their purchases to be added up and bagged. Or they might take it home to respond to later or be surveyed in the car park as they leave.

I recently developed a research questionnaire for a major retailer. When asked, 'Was this store comfortable to be in— not too hot or too cold?' two of the shoppers complained that the stores were cold. Later the management agreed that they themselves had visited their stores to buy personal items in winter and had found the staff 'all rugged up against the cold'.

Now the staff and the customers can look forward to being warm next winter, just from two responses to such a simple (but very important) question.

'I'm glad that we don't have to play in the shade.' Golfer Bobby Jones on being told it was 105 degrees in the shade.

Similarly, I was shopping in Bloomingdales in New York, and the boutique area was so hot I felt sick. As I gave up and left, I commented to the attendant. She said she had been complaining about it for years, but no one would do anything. Her sales were dreadful in the winter because of the heat, and not much better in the summer because of the air-conditioning.

If you are in the professional services industry, send out a survey checking for satisfaction with your clients' accounts. I once used a direct marketing consultancy whose accounting system changed suddenly to billing us progressively throughout the time of the project. The company was so slow in doing the work that the progressive billing was entirely irrelevant; I had not yet seen anything tangible! And since there was no cut-off period, it was hard to figure out what we had paid for and what was still coming in.

If the company concerned had put in a survey form asking if clients were having any trouble with the changeover, the troubles would have eased. They might also have asked if we were satisfied with the work done. I would have told them yes, but that it was done far too slowly. As it was, I just got better and faster at doing more of the projects myself.

KEY POINTS TO REMEMBER

- Choose your prospects wisely through the Commonality Survey. Find out why your competitors' clients are not currently buying from you. Then make sure they do!
- All your prospects in your contact system must be there for very good reasons. Constantly research your clients, customers and prospects for their needs, and meet those needs before your competitors do.

Remember, you are in business to get and keep clients, and thereby make a profit. Getting clients is expensive, losing them is very expensive!

■ ■ ■

Coming next, the single-minded proposition: what quite simply is the benefit of buying your product or service, from the point of view of the person who writes the cheque.

'We all have the strength to endure the misfortunes of others.'
La Rochefoucauld (1613–1680)

GROWTH SKILL 4
THE SINGLE-MINDED PROPOSITION

What quite simply does your company do from your client/customer's point of view? Once you know, you can tell the rest of the world, clearly, loudly **and often.**

A major benefit of hearing from your clients and customers constantly is that these people will help you find the best way to describe your product or service by how they talk about it. Your need for that key phrase becomes evident when you are designing your communications and public relations program.

That key phrase is called either the 'single-minded proposition' or the 'unique selling point'. At Saatchi & Saatchi in Hong Kong, we used to call it the 'simple-minded' proposition, because it stated so simply what the product or service does for the buyer.

Note that I said for the buyer, not for the company selling the product or service. When you have the key phrase down, it will lead you into a corporate statement for all your promotional activities.

'You can find your way across the country using burger joints the way a navigator uses stars.'
Charles Kuralt

If you are having trouble with thinking about the benefits from the point of view of the person paying the bill, think of red roses. The single-minded reason for sending **red** roses (or so I am told in workshops) is sex and guilt. I see no reason to disagree! Yet most florists promote their wares generally and their delivery service primarily.

One memorable day, I did a workshop on the single-minded proposition with an advertising agency. My brief to them was to create the name of and the tag line (from the single-minded proposition) for a business that sold **only** red roses: 24 hours a day, seven days a week, 365 days a year, plus the balloons and cards that went with such a purchase.

Their response? The name was to be 'Bad Boys' and the tag line, based on understanding that red roses were about sex and guilt, was to be, 'We get you into and out of trouble, 24 hours a day.'

See how easy it is to define a tag line when you know why people part with hard-earned money for your product or service? And miraculously, when you are looking for a further example, you see it in the most amazing places. This time it was on a motorway. There it was, a huge poster:

Minolta—we understand the office.

Ever after I have asked my clients, 'What is it that you understand from the buyer's point of view?' and I quote the Minolta example. It becomes but a matter of minutes before you, too, can achieve a similar powerful tag line. In fact, when I am consulting with companies, I ask them to do it just before lunch, and it takes a very few minutes—nothing like hunger to sharpen the mind!

This is so different from the days and weeks that we used to spend thinking, talking, arguing at Saatchi and Saatchi Advertising before we got even close. And recently I saw in a newspaper this advertisement for BMW: 'We understand the blend between man and machine.' Nice one.

'There is never enough time, unless you are serving it.'
Malcolm Forbes

Ask yourself what it is that you understand. If you are in real estate you could say, 'We understand London W1 housing,' or 'We understand New York office space.' If you are a beautician you could say, 'We understand your need to be beautiful.' If you're a lawyer you could say, 'We understand your need for a fair solution.'

An accountant specialising in financial services nominated his single-minded proposition as, 'We understand your need for financial security.'

And Postnet uses, 'We understand your need for a faster, more efficient service.'

Without this thinking about what it is you understand from the buyer's point of view, you get an internal think-tank kind of single-minded proposition. Here's an example: I asked a hotel group what they thought their clients wanted from them. They told me, 'Service that went beyond their expectations.' Had they researched this, I asked, or were they guessing? They said that perhaps they were guessing. The reason I queried their response was that I had recently read a survey that concluded that what guests really cared the most about was cleanliness. If that were missing, then nothing else would make up for it.

Asking around, an associate agreed. He had booked into a good hotel, showered, slept soundly and threw back the sheets to greet the day. Instead he was greeted by dirty black footprints on the bottom sheet, left by the previous occupant.

Another survey, on airlines, showed that what people really cared about was how quickly their luggage came through.

As if to prove the point, recently I travelled from Oman to Dubai with some clients, and as we came out of customs, our luggage was waiting. As if on cue, they said, 'Great journey, there's our luggage.'

Emirates Airlines told me that the Dubai airport has a commitment to getting all luggage out in 13 minutes, versus 25

> 'Do Not Disturb notices should be written in the languages of the hotel maids.'
> **Tim Bedore**

minutes in other parts of the world. And they succeed very well.

So spend time, **really** spend time, listening for the key phrase which will provide the jumping-off point for that simple-minded statement of what it is you provide to your clients or customers. Ring your clients, ask them what it is that you do for them from **their** point of view.

Then when you create any letterhead, business card, literature, leaflet, brochure, annual report, or any item that is bought or seen by the public, be sure to include that simple-minded statement.

Put it in there, boldly and frequently. It tells buyers exactly why they should buy from you, and they will understand your statement because of its simplicity and repetition.

Look around for advertising which shows a clear sense of purpose . . . one which could have come from a 'single-minded proposition'.

'Originality is the art of concealing your sources.'
Unknown

Look around for advertising where the product is presented in the buyers' terms, unfailingly and without deviation. You may not find too many examples, but when you do, they will be powerful.

And work at incorporating your company name into a tag line, the line you will create on hearing from the buying public what it is they think you provide.

For example, if you have a disposable diaper as your product, and the parents say that it keeps their baby free of nappy rash, a linked statement in one typeface like, 'Comfie—the dry one', would help the consumer remember you better than, say, 'The dry one'. The latter statement could be for a beer, a wine, or a clothes dryer.

When you watch ads on TV, see if you can decide what the product is with the sound turned off. If you can, it is a great advertisement; if you can't, it should not be on air.

MAKE THE SINGLE-MINDED PROPOSITION WORK FOR YOU

Write out three quite simple statements that you think express what your company does, from the point of view of the buyer. Imagine that you have paid for a huge highway sign at the cost of $1 million a day. Passing motorists have one second to see your message and go out and buy because of it. Now write to make that $1 million work for you:

1.

2.

3.

Now ring three great clients and ask them what they, quite simply, get from your company. Write in their ideas, statements, comments, whatever.

1.

2.

3.

Example: A client of mine, an advertising agency, discussed what their clients would say about them and decided that it would be 'Argumentative, difficult, stubborn'.

When their head researcher got up the courage to ask the clients he heard, 'The best, committed to excellence, extraordinary attention to the problem, exceptional solutions, great profits.'

Their head researcher took the challenge further, and wrote down what he thought his wife would say about him. He listed, 'Workaholic, never at home, unsupportive, uncaring.'

Then he asked her and heard: 'The best thing that ever happened to me. A great provider, caring and loving, the finest husband and father we could ever have wished for.'

Yes, they did go away on a second honeymoon. It took courage to ask, but note that the rewards were well worth it.

Is there any similarity between what your clients say about you and what you wrote? Would their statements be better on your million dollar poster? Would your clients' comments help you state your speciality so well that many more dollars would flow into your organisation as a result?

If so, use what you have heard to create your all-powerful tag line. Then test that tag line with other clients and prospects.

If it hits the spot, you now have that simple phrase with which to describe why people should buy from you. Use it verbally and in all your corporate literature. Acknowledge the clients and prospects who helped you. Write a letter of thanks, send a gift.

West Coast Coolers provide an example of how an outside person can see things differently. I hear they were developed in this way: Wine growers in California had an excess of wine and asked Faith Popcorn in New York to help them come up with new products.

In a wide-ranging think-tank group, a hairdresser mused, 'Why not add fruit juice to wine, the way we add orange juice to champagne?' The rest is multi-million dollar history.

Here's Woody Allen's single-minded proposition: 'If my films make one more person miserable, I'll have done my job.'

> 'An archaeologist is the best husband a woman can have: the older she gets, the more interested he is in her.'
> **Agatha Christie (1891–1976), who was married to one**

KEY POINTS TO REMEMBER:

- Really work at finding that critical single-minded proposition. It is a three-step process.
- First ask your current clients or customers what it is that they get from you.
- Then when you hear a common theme, create from it a tag line that is directly linked (in the same typeface) with your company name.
- Test that tag line with clients and non-clients. If it makes sense to them, you then use it in all types of written and verbal communication. Example: A prospect asks you why they should see you, and you reply as in the Minolta example, 'Because we understand the office'. Then when someone at a party asks you what you do, you say, 'I understand the office.' Simple, isn't it?

'Advertisements contain the only truths that can be relied upon in a newspaper.'
Thomas Jefferson (1743–1826)

■ ■ ■

The advice to use your single-minded proposition or the tag line (if it is significantly different from the single-minded proposition) in all types of written communication, brings us to the next Growth Skill, which is: 'Look like the company you want to be.'

GROWTH SKILL 5
LOOK LIKE THE COMPANY YOU WANT TO BE

Desks worldwide look about the same: covered with white sheets of paper printed with black ink. It's a lot easier to attract attention if your promotional pieces are bigger, more colourful, and more professional-looking than the many other communications on your prospect's desk.

The fact is that with the right colours, design, copy and layout, you can take a company that was registered today and make it look as stable and as solid as a Rolls-Royce.

Similarly, with different colours, design, copy and layout, you can reposition an older company to look jazzy, exciting and new, if the product has changed sufficiently to warrant such a shift.

It is all what the eye sees in a split second and the brain believes. Now you **can** take control of your corporate look.

COLOUR IN CORPORATE COMMUNICATIONS

All colours have their place, but their effects on us are so immediate that if you use them wrongly, you can destroy the image you're trying to project. If you want to look solid, stable, powerful, royal blue seems to fit the image.

If instead you want to make the recipient feel gentled and cared for by your company's communication, bright red would be too strong. Soft burgundy and gold could be just right.

'Make it simple. Make it memorable. Make it inviting to look at. Make it fun to read.'
Leo Burnett

In my design work I have found that using red and blue together sends out a message of 'solid, stable and secure', plus a hint of danger and excitement. The Pepsi move to blue with red looks very powerful, especially when they paint a Concorde to spread the message!

For you to think about your corporate design, here are some general tips about using colour, gleaned from my years of experience in designing communications for clients:

Pale blue and pale pink are reminiscent of childhood and are often used effectively in catalogues of children's clothing.

Yellow means sunlight, warmth, a lovely day. However, most of us do not see sunlight as yellow, but as enhancing the colours around us. Bright yellow is not a colour many people want to live with; it seems brash in its strongest shades. Thus, yellow (or gold) is better as an accessory to another, more attractive colour; you might use gold leaf on royal blue, burgundy or green.

Strong blue represents solidity and power, stability and security. It is cool and calm and very good to look at. Use it if you are a solid, stable, secure organisation (or wish to look like one).

Green is a colour that surrounds us wherever we go: green trees, green grass, green leaves. Green is peaceful but calls out to be highlighted by an array of vibrant flower colours: red, pink, apricot, yellow or gold. Imagine, for instance, being in a jungle with no tumbling flowers, no highly coloured birds. At first it would be restful, then quite boring.

Brown is earth-coloured, warm, solid, and sensible, but most people do not find it impressive. Avoid using brown to express a corporate identity, unless it is for a caring environmental product.

Red in its blue-red or orange-red tonings is a colour some

'Before you can have a share of market, you must have a share of mind.'
Leo Burnett

love; to others it suggests fire, danger, warlike behaviour and **don't touch**! However, used in moderation or softened to burgundy or maroon, it can be warm and firm at the same time.

Violet, mauve, purple, grey and grey-greens are considered by many to signal mourning, depending on the intensity of the colours. Where a lot of white is added to the above colours, and the effect is silver grey or pale mauve or soft green-grey, the feeling is more of an early morning light. These gentle colours are ideal for expressing soft, emotional products.

Notice what colours influence you to decide that a particular communication comes from a business which knows how to get its message across effectively.

To recap on the subliminal messages of colour, see if you agree with these descriptions:

- Royal blue: Calm, stable, serene, cool, peaceful, trustworthy, restful, honourable.
- Deep red: Warlike, dangerous, hot, passionate, exciting, aggressive, vibrant, prohibitive, stimulating.
- Bright orange: Warm, sensual, joyful, passionate, lively, full of energy, welcoming.
- Yellow: Sunny, cheerful, bright but with an undertone of cowardice and deceit.
- Green: Restful, cool, calm, balanced, fresh, but boring after a while, and also tinged with jealousy.
- Indigo/violet/purple: Royal, dignified, mysterious, powerful, wise, solitary, with strong overtones of control, authority and grief.
- Grey/mauve/grey-green: Sad, old, mournful, withdrawn, lonely, dull, without life or passion.
- Silver grey/pale mauve/light green-grey: Diffusive, gentle, touching, soft.

'If you cannot convince them, confuse them.'
Truman's Law

- Black: Powerful, sophisticated, dramatic, withdrawn, serious, dignified, elegant; yet also sad, evil, wicked and gloomy.
- White: Pure, innocent, youthful, faithful, simple, honest, peaceful.
- Brown: Dirty, dull, boring, unexciting, worthy, uncompromising.

The three primary colours

The three primaries are the boldest, strongest colours. If you ever have trouble remembering what the three primary colours are (the colours from which all other colours grow), simply remember 'ryb', pronounced 'rib', and standing for red, yellow and blue.

Now look into the colours of the rainbow and meet Roy G. Biv = Red, orange, yellow, green, blue, indigo, violet.

To remember the other colours that the primary colours of red, yellow and blue make together is simple: the colour in the middle is created by the two primary colours on either side. Using this, you can recall that red and yellow get together to make orange; yellow and blue mix in to make green; then blue hops around the corner to meet red and out pops indigo or violet, depending on the mix.

You may well ask, why does this matter? It is all to do with creating the point of greatest contrast: you use colours that stand out against the background to draw the eye of the reader to your single-minded statement or powerful graphic design, be it on a brochure, flyer, advertisement, or point of sale.

The primary colours, red, yellow and blue, and the secondary colour of orange (mixed from red and yellow) are the most intense and make a good background for your contrasting colours.

Primary colours as background

Let's imagine royal blue as your brochure background colour; white stands out against it more dramatically than any other colour. Now take red as a background; again white stands out against it vividly. Take yellow or orange as a background colour; black stands out well, better than white would.

Primary colours as foreground

If we reverse all this and have a background of white, we find that blue, red and black stand out well. Against a background of black yellow, orange and white stand out well. Playing around further, we can see that black on dark blue disappears, yellow on red does not work very well (these colours almost seem to 'eat' each other up) and red and black together looks a bit dull.

A shining black car is seen as powerful and deadly, a shining white car as pure and clean. (Consider a black funeral car v. a white wedding car.) A shiny or dull black brochure gives a lethal message. A shiny or even flat white brochure expresses purity instantly. These two 'colours' give out more immediate and clearer messages than any other colour.

Secondary colours for your corporate image

Let's recap on the secondary colours: orange, green, indigo/violet. Could we use these as background or foreground colours? Yes indeed, if they represent the imagery we want to express.

An orange brochure would look good with contrasted colours such as black, blue, green or white. A green brochure could look great incorporating flower colours such as apricot, orange, gold, red.

And indigo/violet is so close to blue that red, orange and yellow would be good contrasts. The field is open to whatever

'I don't know the key to success, but the key to failure is trying to please everybody.'
Bill Cosby

you want to use, providing you are satisfied that the image sent out represents your company.

You will notice that the contrasting colours which work well are the ones with the opposite degree of warmth.

The warm colours of red, orange and yellow contrast well with the cool colours of green, blue, indigo and violet. No need to struggle with what goes with what. Just choose two that look good together in terms of intense contrast and they will automatically be the cool and the warm.

As for white and black, the cool shades of green and the three blues (royal, indigo and violet) go well with white, providing they are enhanced by touches of warm colours; the warm shades of yellow, orange and red go well with black.

The reverse does not work so well when you try to put cool with cool, warm with warm. Green with black, or blue with black, cannot create enough contrast to immediately attract the eye.

Similarly, yellow with white is too close to create a powerful contrast. Orange, which is made with the two warm colours, red and yellow, and has an incredible strength of its own, works brilliantly with black and very well with white.

Green, on the other hand, is made with one warm and one cool colour (yellow and blue) so it does not have that intensity of effect on the eye and the mind and needs a lot of support from other warmer colours to remain attractive to the viewer.

With any colour, if you want to pale its intensity, add white. Red loses its strength to become pink, orange mutes down to apricot, yellow weakens to cream, green becomes insipid, blue is washed out, indigo and violet are muted to remind one of dark shadows, and black becomes grey. Mix up the three primaries (red, yellow and blue) and you get brown.

The eye will obey your command

If the basic colour of your brochure is royal blue and you use a large block of big, white type against it, the eye will go immediately to that point of greatest contrast. The eye obeys, it simply cannot help itself.

In this instance, if you have a secondary message, make its white print slightly smaller than the first bold white message and the eye will go there next. However, if you use dark blue with black print, that will be the last thing the eye will see.

White waves against a dark blue sky; a rich red rock against a pale blue sky—these stand out vividly. Imagine handkerchiefs of light and dark shades in a dark suit pocket and see for yourself how strongly the light handkerchief draws your eye.

Use your single-minded proposition on all your printed material

When you have your single-minded proposition, use this design technique to make that message stand out on your brochure or flyer.

For example, International Courier Brokers decided that their single-minded proposition was, 'We understand your courier needs, nationally and internationally.' When we designed their new corporate ID, we made good use of that proposition on their letterhead, business cards, envelopes and other stationery, using red and blue on white.

SOLID AND STABLE OR BRIGHT AND JAZZY?

It is so important to get your image right at first glance. Decide whether you want to be solid and long-lasting, or bright, jazzy and new. When you have made that decision, here is how you effectively present your new image:

'If you look like your passport photo, you're too ill to travel.'
Will Kommen

The location of your wording and graphics is important. Place them on the right side of the front cover of your corporate brochure and you're seen as powerful and long-lasting.

Put the same wording or graphics on the left side and you're seen as young, snappy and fresh. The reason for this is that what is seen on the right-hand side of the page is acknowledged by the left-hand, analytical side of the brain. Similarly, what is seen on the left-hand side of the page goes through to the right-hand, creative side of the brain. Colours have a similar impact: jazzy fluorescent colours give a completely different impression from solid, sensible colours.

'Ideas alone enable a man to survive and flourish.'
Leo Burnett

Test your designs on clients and prospects. Ask them for their first-glance impressions. The value of the 'what is it?' question is that it is a non-defensive enquiry. You are genuinely interested in hearing their answers. If the response is negative at any time, do not defend yourself; simply keep asking 'what is it?' questions.

(You can transfer this 'what is it?' technique to other personal and business aspects of your life. It is an excellent negotiating technique, because you get real answers. You no longer have to second-guess the issues.)

By placing copy in the proper position and using the best colours for your purpose, you can ensure the harmony of your communications, and ensure that they are read and understood.

Use the best quality paper for corporate communications. Everything that looks cheap says 'cheap' about you. Everything you do well is to your credit ever after.

Brochures look best with a glossy finish, whereas smooth, matt paper is best for your letterhead. A company's written pieces reflect the personality and operating philosophy of the owners and managers which, like it or not, is forcefully passed on to the reader.

THE GOLDEN LINE

About 2000 years ago, the Greek mathematician Pythagoras said that there was a natural law and order of design in life, and he called it 'The Golden Mean'. For the sake of design simplicity, we will call it the Golden Line.

When you look at something beautiful, like a Vermeer painting, a Georgian house or a piece of jewellery in just the right spot on a coat, chances are that it is on the Golden Line. Using the Golden Line is simple and it makes your printed material look terrific. It is based on thirds.

This is how to do it:

Step One: Take a plain sheet of paper (the size of your normal letters) and fold it in half across the centre, **horizontally.**

Step Two: Open the paper flat and fold the top edge down twice equally to the centre line, **horizontally.** This divides the top half of the paper into three equal sections above the centre.

Repeat from the bottom edge, so the paper is ultimately divided into six equal sections, three above the centre line and three below it. These are your **horizontal Golden Lines.**

Step Three: Open the paper flat again and fold it **vertically** in thirds. Thus, you will have divided the page into equal thirds from one side to the other. Each of those thirds is a Golden Line on the **vertical.**

Your page will have folded oblong boxes, made from the vertical and horizontal folds, which you now can use as guidelines to lay out the key elements of your letterhead, brochure, flyer and anything else you have in mind.

Use the vertical left third of the sheet or the right third for your key messages: your company name and address and your single-minded statement about your product. Leave the

> 'We are what we pretend to be.'
> **Kurt Vonnegut, Jr.**

centre blank. The eye likes white space, so create as much of it as you can.

Each of the Golden Line oblongs has mini-thirds within. So you can either work within your major Golden Line oblongs or you can go outside of the major lines to the mini-lines.

Similarly, you can fold the bottom third of the page into thirds again and use the middle third for your company address and details. Do not use the very bottom third, because faxes often lose that space.

You can use this technique to create a corporate image for yourself which, by the very pleasure of looking at it, expresses a harmony and style which says so much about you.

Fold your current letterhead as described above, and see whether your company name and address fits on or inside the Golden Line boxes you have created with your folded lines. If not, try shifting the detail until it looks harmonious to you, using the Golden Line boxes as guidelines.

Try not to use the centre for words or graphics when designing a brochure or flyer front cover. The brain can't get a fix on information in the centre position. It needs to see things on the left or right side in order to decide whether you are bright, jazzy and new or solid, stable and secure.

A look of harmony is usually based on the thirds of the Golden Line, so leave the centre as a peaceful space in front cover design and see how often you can leave peaceful centre space inside your brochure, also.

'If you have the facts on your side and honest conviction in your heart, you rarely lose by fighting for your idea all the way.'
Leo Burnett

When using the vertical third lines to position your corporate statements, remember that on the right third, the message is seen as powerful, solid and stable; on the left third: jazzy, exciting and new.

The Golden Lines can guide you throughout any publication, any piece of literature that has to be designed.

Before I begin to write any copy, I lay out the vertical and the horizontal Golden Lines. Then I look at the brochure from a left-hand/right-hand side of the brain point of view.

Are we to be seen as solid and well established or exciting and innovative?

If the first, I use the right-hand side of the page for the important points I want to make. If the latter, I move all the important words over to the left side. Power statements can look good on both sides; the choice of one or the other is a matter of the type of company you wish to portray.

For instance, I have a corporate brochure here with me as I write this. The company concerned is very solid, stable and international. They have listed all their international offices and addresses in small, small print down the left-hand side of the front cover of their brochure.

If they moved their international offices and addresses over to the right-hand side and stacked them top to bottom down the lower two-thirds of the front cover, pointing to their single minded proposition, the power of the piece would be far greater, especially if done in larger print as well.

Currently it is thin and weak and, being on the left-hand side of the page, goes through to the right-hand, creative side of the brain, sending out the message of weak and creative rather than big and strong and internationally stable.

LOOK AROUND FOR EFFECTIVE EXAMPLES

Getting the right look to your corporate materials will help you win appointments. Prospects will make snap judgements based on how your 'window-dressing' looks to them. You will survive and prosper if their gut reaction is in your favour. Analyse your own gut reactions to material.

'Work is of two kinds: first, altering the position of matter at or near the earth's surface relative to other matter; second, telling other people to do so.'
Bertrand Russell (1872–1970)

Go through all the possible places in your work area where old brochures and flyers might collect, on any product whatsoever. Pull them out and take them to a quiet place for your research.

Ring up every company you have ever thought of investing in through the share market and ask for their end-of-year financial report.

Clip coupons and send off for catalogues of every kind.

Go into car showrooms and take their brochures, especially the top-of-the-line cars.

Go into travel companies and take the brochures that make you want to leave town and the ones that make you want to stay home. Take the good, the bad and the ugly.

Collect, look, analyse, feel, read everything you can lay your hands on. Then compare your present corporate look with the way you would like it to be next time you print new material. You will find that you now have a naturally trained eye, that quality attracts and ugliness repels.

THE CONTENTS OF YOUR LETTER

'There is no pleasure in having nothing to do. The fun is having lots to do and not doing it.'
John W. Raper

A good letter has a beginning, a middle and an end. First, tell recipients why you want them to read the letter. Next, tell them what you want them to know. Close by telling them what action will come next: that you will call them for an appointment; that they should fill in an enclosed form if they would like to buy your product; that they should call or reply by a certain date, etc.

Assume the recipients of your letter are busy and tired. Don't write a letter that leaves them wondering why you wrote or what they should do to get what you're offering. Make it easy for people to continue the relationship with you.

Don't use flowery language. The message in the words, 'He

was delayed by the breakdown of his motor vehicle' is more easily conveyed to busy people as, 'His car broke down, so he was late.' People respect easy, clear communications.

If you want readers to continue onto a second or third page, make sure to end the page in mid-sentence, so the reader has to turn over to complete the message. This is an old Reader's Digest technique and it works.

THE APPEARANCE OF YOUR LETTER

How do you get your letter read? Keep it simple and short. Think of any printed communication as having three elements:

1. The coastline (the shape of the words)
2. The land mass (the size of the paragraphs)
3. The sky and ocean (the white spaces surrounding the paragraphs).

We read words by the shape of their letters, by their coastline. In a word like 'pretty' there is an interesting coastline between the p, the t's and the y, which makes it an easily recognisable word. Now try to read this: PRETTY.

See how much more difficult it is to read all in capitals? That is because we now have to read each letter separately, instead of speeding across a known shape. Our reading is slowed down considerably as a result, so never use capitals in body text.

<u>Underlining, too, makes words almost completely illegible.</u> When you want someone to take notice of what you have written, put the words you want **to stand out in bold, heavy type.**

The human eye (and mind) likes peace. It likes lots of white space. It is no accident that most stationery is restful white or cream-coloured. Leave big margins left and right. Have small paragraphs of no more than sixty words. That's six lines of ten words.

'Writing is easy. All you do is stare at a blank sheet of paper until drops of blood form on your head.'
Gene Fowler (1890–1960)

Write short sentences and simple words. Use a typeface that has serifs, which are short, curved or straight cross-lines at the top and bottom of most of its letters. Serifs help us decipher the letters; that's why newspapers, magazines and this book use type faces with serifs.

People read most easily the way they read most commonly. Since the preferred reading for pleasure is usually newspapers and magazines and we are therefore used to the serif typefaces used in these publications, make sure you use a serif typeface when you go to print. It can be useful, too, to publish reports and copies of speeches in double columns, as in magazines.

When a glance at your printed page shows lots of sky and ocean and little land mass, you have a communication that people will want to read. The same usually applies to advertising. Use lots of white space, a few precise words and images and you're a winner.

'He writes so well he makes me feel like putting my quill back in my goose.'
Fred Allen
(1894–1956)

MAKE GOOD-LOOKING LETTERS HAPPEN IN YOUR ORGANISATION

Check the appearance and content of your letters. Go to your filing basket or cabinet and pull out at random a handful of recent letters sent to clients, prospects, suppliers, debtors, creditors, whomever. Imagine receiving these letters yourself and ask these questions:

Are the letters excellent communications at first glance by virtue of quality paper, typeface and printing? Do your company name, logo and address stand out clearly? Can people easily find your phone, fax and Email details?

I had a client in America whose letterhead and invoices were so muddled that they received letters and cheques made out to their prominently stated street address! Their company name was lost among their overseas affiliates.

Are the letters well laid out, with small paragraphs, big margins, good space between the paragraphs? Does the letter look peaceful and welcoming at first glance?

Are all the sentences clear in their intent and content? Are the spelling and grammar correct? Are simple words used throughout? Does the reader know why you have written and what is to be done next? Is the tone pleasant and helpful? Did you make a friend in every case by sending these letters?

Now you may wish to look at your incoming mail and see how many pieces meet these basic standards. Perhaps you will see some really good examples of great-looking and great-sounding letters from your associates; then again, you may realise that you are well ahead of the average.

'I don't want any yes-men around me. I want everybody to tell me the truth even if it costs them their jobs.'
Sam Goldwyn,
(1882–1974)

DRESS FOR SUCCESS

One of my great pleasures in a workshop is passing around magazine pictures of men and women in various kinds of business and casual dress. Participants are asked to check or cross whether they would buy from this person or not.

Without exception the whole room wants to buy from the man in the Dunhill look: the navy blue blazer, the crisp white shirt and the red and blue striped tie. No other look will do.

I mentioned this to the head of a financial planning company, investing for high net-worth individuals, and he remarked with delight that their best-selling consultant dresses exactly like that every day of his working life. And every day he sells more and more. He is only 29, yet is far ahead of many older and more experienced staff.

The preferred look for women is white, black and white, navy, navy and white, royal blue and white and cream. I now wear just those colours. Apart from looking more business-like, I know exactly what I need to pack for a trip.

KEY POINTS TO REMEMBER

- Decide whether your company should look solid, stable and secure or bright, jazzy and new. Then design on the Golden Line, choose relevant colours and position your copy with the left brain/right brain difference in mind to immediately give a congruent impression.

- NEVER USE CAPITALS FOR BODY TEXT. They are difficult to read, and people won't read your message. Why are they difficult to read? Because CAPITALS/capitals take away the shape of a word as you can see above. No longer does the word have a coastline; it is just a block of copy.

   When we are very young we read letter by letter— c a t—but as we get better at reading we read 'cat' by the coastline of the word.

- To get attention, **put it in bold instead. With no underlining, because being bold is enough.**

   People read most easily in the way they read most commonly: books, magazines and newspapers use lower case except for some headings. Use wide margins, short paragraphs, simple words. Have a beginning, a middle and an end to all your communications.

   For my own letterhead, and for two clients, I am now using only the right-hand side two thirds of the page, leaving the left-hand side empty and therefore available for a handwritten message, drawing attention to the key message in the copy. Then when I ring a prospect and ask if they received my letter, I remind them that it has a handwritten note in the margin. Instant recall!

'If you look good and dress well, you don't need a purpose in life.'
Fashion consultant Robert Pante

■ ■ ■

Growth Skill 6 will show you how to be at your best on the telephone and just when your regular, relentless contacting will pay off.

GROWTH SKILL 6
SUCCESS IN YOUR CALLING CYCLES

GETTING THOSE APPOINTMENTS

With the cost of a single face-to-face visit being estimated at $2,600—whether or not you get the sale—your primary method of contacting prospects should be by phone.

And that phone call should be a follow-up to a well-designed and interesting communication, sent previously. We need to remember that our clients and prospects are overwhelmed with responsibilities and awash with distracting and often irrelevant information.

Even if they like you and love what you can do for them, the pressures of daily life will keep them from focusing on you.

And remember, if they do say 'no', they may well mean, 'no, not now,' not, 'no' forever. And they are only saying no to the opportunity, not to you.

Avoid falling in love with the names or reputations of particular companies. Instead, fall in love with the number of companies you are going to contact. Achieve a high volume of prospects—a minimum of 200 per new-business person on staff—and keep in touch regularly and relentlessly.

Don't promise yourself that prospect number eighteen is the one you're going to win. That deflects your attention from the whole, just as dreaming of all the money you're going to make fogs up your mind when you're meant to be listening to

> 'Nature has given us two ears but only one mouth.'
> **Benjamin Disraeli (1804–1881)**

a prospect's needs. Remember, a sale is not a sale until the cheque is cleared through the bank, and commitments made are as liable to change as they are in your own life.

Determining who is the right person to talk to within an organisation may be the most difficult and time-consuming aspect of your new-business campaign.

Trying to reach the individual responsible for purchasing the goods or services you offer can be a long and tedious process, but it will save you time and money in the future.

Because the decision is often made by several people, you must start at the top of the organisation so the real decision-maker knows of you, and then keep that person informed as you deal with the other staff that he or she has nominated. The Japanese have a model for this; it is called the double figure of eight, where they go top to bottom through an organisation and from side to side.

Then people from the bottom and across middle management, as well as at the top, know about your product or service, and are more likely therefore to agree.

You know about the one bad apple in the barrel rotting all the other apples; well, one negative person in the room can override all the others.

I asked a class why this is possible, and their reply was that you always think the person who disagrees has better, more recent knowledge, so you give in. So true! Recall how often you were going to a favourite restaurant and someone said not to go, it had gone off. Immediately you believed that they must have better, more up-to-date experience.

The gatekeeper

'Gatekeepers' are the assistants or secretaries who screen calls and decide whether to put you through to the boss.

They're a necessary part of the process. A lot of people think the gatekeeper is just someone you have to get around. The reality is that you're going to be coming into contact with gatekeepers over and over again. It's a mistake to treat these people lightly.

Gatekeepers talk with the boss; they are able to give the boss an impression of who you are. If you are pleasant, well prepared and patient, all of that will be conveyed to the boss. Gatekeepers can be wonderfully helpful, or they can slow things up and keep you from getting to the main person.

'There is no human problem which could not be solved if people would simply do as I advise.'
Gore Vidal

THE CALLING CYCLES

As stressed, a three-month call cycle (or less) must be established. Never go longer than three months without calling. Make sure that the conversation is friendly, courteous, polite and non-demanding. You are building a relationship of trust, not one of war.

You can make contact again **before** three months have elapsed if you wish, but contact and recontact your two hundred or so prospects without fail at least once within each 90-day period.

If you follow this schedule and move daily through your list, whether you reach the party or not, you will need to average only three to four calls per day on a list of about two hundred prospects and clients . . . If you don't reach a particular prospect after two attempts, give up phoning until the next three-month cycle unless you have something really important to say now, in which case you keep on trying.

If not, create a relationship by sending a handwritten note or greeting card saying: 'Sorry that I missed you. If I may, I'll be in touch again within three months.' Enclose your business card and be in touch again, within three months or less.

If you do not get through next time, send another note and another and another, until you do get through. (See section on 'Saying thank you in a memorable way' for advice on the type and quality of card on which to write your note.)

The first cycle

In my experience, the first time you make the phone calls to your contacts, you quite quickly get some business. It's called beginner's luck. There are always firms that are unhappy with their existing supplier and will say yes just to establish a new relationship.

However, in general you'll find that your chances of getting an appointment from the first cold letter or phone call are about one-half to one per cent. So, from 200 prospects, you might get one or two appointments the first time around (but beginner's luck can mean that you get five or 10 or 20; then sadly it doesn't last, and you go back to the norm, as follows).

To all those who say 'No', you will say, 'Thank you' and also, 'If you don't mind, we'll be in touch again in three months' time.' Don't be discouraged; just as life changes, so does business. When needs change and your product or service is required, you will be favoured over the casual cold caller because your prospect has grown to trust you. That means you get the business. Prospects don't mean 'No'; they mean 'Not now'.

'If called by a panther, don't anther.'
Ogden Nash,
(1902–1971)

The second cycle

Within three months, you write and/or phone again, just as you said you would. Your percentage of appointments is likely to rise to about two or 3 per cent—maybe a total of six appointments from your 200 contacts.

The third cycle

Three months later, at the ninth month, write and/or phone again. Now, because you have been in regular contact, the prospect has learned to trust you. You didn't give up the first or second time: you came back. In the third cycle, your appointments are likely to rise to around 7 to 10 per cent—perhaps 14 to 20 appointments from the 200 prospects.

The fourth cycle: things begin to happen

Beginning with the fourth cycle, the percentages will increase dramatically and you may find about 30 per cent of your prospects will agree to an appointment.

The fifth cycle: things are really happening!

Be well prepared for success by the fifth cycle, as you can secure appointments and buying signals from up to 60 per cent of your well-chosen prospects. Keep on keeping on and you will get up to 80 per cent of your prospects turning into clients.

Here's another speaker, trainer, consultant who agrees. At a recent conference for an insurance company, I spoke about how to grow your business, and put particular emphasis on the amazing success that arrives at the fifth cycle of contacting and re-contacting your wide band of well-chosen prospects, within the 90-day cycle.

The next speaker was Bill Gibson from Canada and he, too, said, that it is from the fifth contact and beyond that you will get up to 82% acceptance of your product or service. So there were two of us who had seen and heard the positive results, and similar statistics, from simply following up.

My figures about the percentage of positive responses you

> If I had my life to live again, I would make the same mistakes, only sooner.'
> **Tallulah Bankhead (1902–1968)**

get in each cycle are on the conservative side. People often tell me that they get a level of response higher than my predictions. If you're able to do better, terrific!

However, start off comfortably, assuming you will do as well as this model suggests. Fewer positive responses may be a sign that you have to change or improve the look or sound of your message, or that you need a stronger, more frequent effort to maintain a regular stream of prospects.

A LITTLE RESEARCH IS ENOUGH

'Great moments in science: Einstein discovers that time is actually money.'
Gary Larson cartoon caption

Entrepreneurs often paralyse themselves by doing too much research. They sit around for hours, days, weeks, tracking down what they consider to be relevant information about an organisation, using the research as an excuse not to pick up that phone.

In essence, most of the research is a waste of time because whatever information you can gather is usually out of date by the time you get it.

All that 'knowledge' can set you up for a bad appointment, because prospects love to talk about themselves, and if you go to a meeting full of information, you may not listen. You may be presupposing and presuming and you even may be bored with everything the prospect is going to tell you.

A small amount of research is enough, something that might take you a couple of hours, such as phoning to request an annual report, and then reading it.

Simply call a gatekeeper and say, 'Would you mind helping me? I'm trying to get a little more information about your company. Could you send me a copy of your annual report?'

For privately held companies, ask for brochures and any other information they distribute. Use this opportunity to build a relationship with the gatekeeper, and when the annual report and brochures you requested are received, call back or write a note to say thank you.

When you arrive for your meeting, your prospect will be aware that you've done some homework. Then ask intelligent questions and listen with genuine interest.

Don't ever be afraid of cold calling. After the first successful contact, your prospects become warm calls.

Review your list of around two hundred prospects. It is possible that you did not get two hundred. The reason most people give is that they 'know' many of their likely prospects have a long history of being tied to another company, so their prospect numbers dropped back considerably.

May I suggest that you put these people back on your list. You will never know until you try whether a prospect is going to become a client. Everything changes. Even the most committed business relationship can fail for all the usual reasons that personal relationships fail.

One of my clients put aside Friday afternoons to work everything out. His prospect list grew a little longer every Friday until he got his two hundred.

All the information was in the computer; he had a modem so that the phone numbers were dialled at the push of a button; a large box of good-looking cards was at his side for those 'Sorry that I missed you when I rang' notes. He was determined not to do too much research and to make at least four to six calls a day.

And it worked. He told me he made a second call to a prospect, three months later, and she said to please come in, adding that he was the only person who had ever called back when he said he would. So it doesn't take much to be ahead of the game.

Those note-cards are of key importance. Playing telephone tag is frustrating. By handwriting a note and sending it off

'Do it big or stay in bed.'
Opera producer Larry Kelly

each time you cannot contact the prospect, you 'shift the monkey' right out of the way. Otherwise, you end up with so many calls to do you feel tempted to give up.

An idea for those of us with not-so-good handwriting: use the thickish felt tip calligraphy pens. They make the handwriting look so much clearer and stronger. But do let the ink dry before closing your note or greeting card; otherwise it smudges and you have to start all over again.

COLD CALLING

'I have a new philosophy. I am only going to dread one day at a time.'
Charles Schulz

Why are we so afraid to make cold calls? The fear of rejection? We don't want to spoil our day by doing things which might not work. You bet!

All that is needed to overcome the distaste of making cold calls is a slightly different perspective: the view that new-business development is a numbers game.

So, if we have 200 contacts, we know that somewhere out there is somebody who's going to say 'yes'. We just have to get there by way of a lot of, 'No, not now.'

As Saatchi's David Miln says, 'Those who make three times more phone calls than their competitors are four times more successful.'

Considering that almost no one consistently makes new-business phone calls, being three times better than your competitors is easy!

Everyone experiences ups and downs in business. If you get appointments with your first few phone calls, you may think, 'This is easy, anyone can do new business.'

Then you go into a long, low time when all you hear are those deadly excuses: every person you call is busy, is interstate, on holidays, out of the office, in a meeting, will call you back, or simply does not want to see you.

Get over the pain by getting back on the phone, trotting along like a marathon runner, just getting the 'Yes, please come in' or the 'No, not now'. Yeses and noes are the prospect's choice. They will say 'yes' to you when they are ready.

The longer, harder and smarter you work, the luckier you get. In London it was said that business was done two months of the year, but no one knew which two months. In New York getting appointments was so tough it was the equivalent of winning the war in the Middle East.

Then I found that in New York business was done one month of the year, in August when 'everyone' was out of town. Those who were left behind were delighted to see people.

Outside of New York, everyone was willing to see you, but then one had to travel in order to reach them and that was impressive enough to get you the appointment.

In Australia and South Africa it seems to be year-round business, with exceptions such as the end of the financial year, school holidays and Christmas/New Year. And although I find appointments relatively easy to get in South Africa, the decisions take just as long as they do everywhere else in the world.

'The two hardest things to handle in life are failure and success.' **Unknown**

In Hong Kong, Singapore, Malaysia and Thailand I found business was done every hour of every day, except in August when the European side of business went quiet with the expatriates away on holidays. Other than that, business went on as normal, night and day.

And in the end, why do people buy? Because of greed, fear and laziness. If you can meet some or all of those needs, you will likely have a quicker decision.

How do you get going?

First of all, you must develop a contact card, or have all the information on the computer screen:

- Name and title of the person you're calling
- Name of this person's gatekeeper (if you don't know it, find out)
- Correct company name and address
- Correct telephone, fax and Email numbers
- Company's industry
- Company's size by staff and revenue

From research you should also have:

(a) The knowledge to choose a wide band of likely prospects, all of whom will one day need your product or service. The commonality survey is your guideline here.

(b) The 'single-minded proposition'—the reason your clients chose you and stay with you, so that you can clearly tell your prospects the one major benefit of choosing to use your product or service.

No need to confuse them; just give them one valid reason, from their point of view, why they should meet with you.

Remember, they won't give up their time to discuss their needs with you unless they can foresee a major benefit.

Take the card in your hand or bring up the information on your computer screen and dial the phone number. Ask to speak to the person whom you have identified as the top decision-maker in the organisation. It is easy to work down through an organisation, but it is extremely difficult to work up.

Remember, it is always best to write to and ask for one of the top titles: chairman, president, chief executive officer, chief financial officer. If you're later told to call someone further down the organisational hierarchy, at least you've made contact with a senior executive to whom you can refer.

Try to enlist the gatekeeper's help.

If you have mailed a letter and information, enquire whether

'Every morning I get up and look through the Forbes list of the richest people in America. If I am not there, I go to work.'

Robert Orben

your mailing has been received. If there is no memory of it, re-mail the package, but addressed to the gatekeeper personally, for the attention of the boss. Wait several days, call the gatekeeper again and say, 'Did you receive our package?'

If yes, ask, 'Have you been able to pass it on yet? Do you know when (the boss) would like to meet with me?'

The incidence of appointments after re-mailing and enlisting the help of the gatekeeper is often very high, providing you have a simple way of explaining what your product or service will do for them . . . what is unique about you. (See the chapter on the single-minded proposition.)

Another valuable technique is to get the name of the gatekeeper and fax that person for their boss, explaining that you will be in the area at a certain time on a certain day and will visit unless it is inconvenient for them.

You will always get a response, as they don't want you turning up if they are not going to be there, particularly if you are travelling interstate to see them. If the time is not convenient, you can negotiate another mutually suitable time. Now you have an appointment around which to base your next visit to the area.

To achieve total memory recall for my client in America, I had the envelopes overprinted with a band of royal blue down the side. Inside the envelope was a royal blue folder and cream letterhead with the company name in gold foil. The supporting information was done on cream paper with—yes, you've guessed it—a royal blue line down the side.

We got a lot of comments about the integrated and professional look of our mailing piece and a lot of appointments, too. And everyone we phoned remembered receiving the big white envelope with the royal blue line down the side.

Recently, in another country, I was showing this big white envelope with its blue line when my client started to laugh

> 'It takes a great person to be a good listener.'
> **Arthur Helps**
> **(1813–1875)**

and shake his head. I asked why and he said it was so amazingly simple and yet so effective that it was unbelievable. Yes, it is really that simple to be noticed in the mail.

Cold calls can be the best part of your day

Learn to like cold calling. You would die of exhaustion if everyone said 'yes' to an appointment, so love those 'noes'. I ask people to physically leap up and say 'Hurrah, I got a "no", so now I don't have to go out in the rain/cold/heat/noise . . .' and really mean it.

You can also moan and groan when you get a 'yes' if you like, because now you do have to go out in the rain/cold/heat/noise etc.

See cold calling as the easiest part of your day. With this system, cold calling is simple because if people are not in, you simply write a note and keep moving. To increase your chances of a personal contact, start early in the day, around eight o'clock. You will often find people in between twelve and one in the afternoon and between five and six in the evening.

Remember to use the fax and enrol the gatekeeper when you really want an appointment. You can speak to the gatekeeper, ask permission to send a fax, explain your reasons for needing the appointment, list your free times and continue to liaise with her.

You may never speak to the senior person until the day of the appointment, but you will surely get it organised.

Look good to yourself when you're making phone calls. With more and more people working from home, the temptation can be to dress down for the occasion.

Try this for a test. One morning dress in your best business outfit and start making calls. Then change to an old tracksuit and see if you feel as great.

Any sense of self-worth comes out in your voice; similarly, any self-doubt.

UNDERSTANDING THE PERSON ON THE OTHER END

(My thanks to British Telecom for their notes from which this section is taken.)

Most people fall into one of four personal styles. Each of these types requires a different response from you if you are to be successful in getting appointments.

However, don't be too quick to judge people by how they sound on the phone. There are too many unknown elements to a phone conversation: you cannot see the other person and you don't know what kind of day he or she has had.

Stay relaxed and listen; allow an image of the speaker to drift into your mind. You will find that such an impression can often prove remarkably accurate.

For instance, allowing for regional variations, a rapid rate of rational speech generally shows above-average intelligence. Hesitation, stammering, and pauses may suggest anxiety or indecisiveness, or that you are talking to the wrong person.

Generally, you will be able to figure out how to conduct your conversation by using language that fits with the following four personality styles, mentioned earlier.

Aspirers use the language of achievement and are often entrepreneurs in their own business. They speak about setting goals, working towards objectives, planning and thinking ahead, making progress and moving onward.

'I never know how much of what I say is true.'
Bette Midler

Their tone is brisk, business-like and purposeful. They will finish your sentences, interrupt you and end the call abruptly. Don't assume they are in the office when you speak to them. They could well be at home, in a car, on a train or a plane.

They are forever moving around, setting their goals and going forward.

Aspirers want callers to be brisk, direct, organised and straight to the point. If you waste their time, you will be unpopular. Have a clear idea of what you want from the call before phoning.

Stress how your ideas can help Aspirers to attain goals or make more efficient use of their time. Don't bother them with details.

Give the whole picture, prices, benefits and availability in one quick statement. If you follow up by fax, electronic or voice mail, you will impress them.

Show yourself to be quick, accurate, and efficient. If they like your style, you'll get their business.

'When ideas fail, words come in handy.'
Goethe

Enquirers act like accountants (and often are), saying things like: 'Let's consider the facts . . .', 'Speaking objectively . . .', 'Logical thinking requires . . .', 'The way I see it . . .', and 'I think it is important that we do it this way'.

They speak slowly, reflecting carefully on their words and instantly correcting any mistakes they consider you've made.

They let ideas sink in for a long time before they reply and before they commit themselves, leaving you to face long silences.

Enquirers do not like social chat. Just provide relevant facts and figures. If you don't know the answer, say so immediately and honestly. Don't guess.

Say you'll find out, say you'll phone back. Speak firmly, unemotionally, clearly and precisely.

It's a good idea to send Enquirers a fax or letter covering all the key points in your conversations, so that they continue to be impressed by your efficiency. When Enquirers have enough facts, they will trust you with just one project, not an entire job. When you've proved yourself, you will get the job.

Admirers often use phrases like 'My feeling about this is . . .', or 'My intuition tells me that . . .', or 'I sense that . . .'. They speak quietly and calmly.

They listen carefully to what you say. There may be sudden long silences that make you think the phone has broken down. It hasn't; they're just quietly and genuinely listening to you. Their preferred role in an organisation is in human resources.

Admirers want business calls to be sociable. They like to chat about friends, families, holidays, sports, or the weather. Take time to listen to their ideas or problems and be warm and caring about them. Admirers use their silences to coax you into revealing information about yourself, your business and your feelings—perhaps even more than you may have intended to tell them.

When they are sure that you are 'one of them' and they determine that your service will benefit the people in their organisation, you will get their business.

Inspirers are visionaries and often heads of large organisations. They love words that convey great energy. They say things like 'It sounds great . . .', 'This is an amazing project . . .', 'I am delighted by the idea . . .', 'You're going to love this'. They will cut you short when they get bored with the conversation. Their closing phrases are words like 'Fine, fine . . .', 'Right . . .', 'Okay . . .', when they mean 'Goodbye'.

They talk quickly and urgently, with ideas tumbling excitedly over one another, such is their speed of delivery. Being at the top in a big way, they hate detail, but love big pictures.

Inspirers get bored quickly. They need variety in conversations; so don't be afraid of introducing several different topics or jumping from one idea to the next.

Speak in a lively, enthusiastic manner that conveys urgency and excitement about what you're doing.

'Anyone who says they can see through women is missing a lot.'
Groucho Marx (1895–1977)

Inspirers also respond with delight to a 'thank you' expressed in a quick note or a simple phone call. Keep Inspirers entertained and you will have their business.

TALKING TO THE SENIOR EXECUTIVE

'Nobody can make you feel inferior without your consent.'
Eleanor Roosevelt (1884–1962)

Sometimes you will get straight through to the senior executive with whom you want to speak, often if you phone between 8 and 9 a.m., at lunch time or after 5 p.m. If you're not prepared, you may be left thinking, 'Help! I didn't mean to speak to this person. I meant to have a long, ongoing relationship with the secretary to save me from an appointment I'm rather nervous about.'

If it happens that you get to speak directly with someone who says, 'Yes, I got your package and, yes, I do want to see you,' be ready to respond appropriately.

Negotiate a suitable time; write or fax immediately so that the person has it in writing. Call the day before to confirm. I call again on the day itself to reconfirm, as often something has come up to delay the other person, and a useless journey is saved.

In the meeting realise that the other person may be nervous too. Remember your probing techniques and ask 'what is it?' questions to find out what their real needs are. If they have given up their time to meet with you, they usually have a need.

It is over to you to probe gently, focusing on their needs. Do not try to respond with instant-fix answers. After the meeting, remember to say and to write thank you to everyone who helped you and saw you. The important thing is to send off your note of thanks as soon as possible after the day of the appointment, preferably that evening or at the latest, the next day.

Within three to five days of the meeting, you should, as

promised, come back with some suggestions on how your company can help, having given real time to thinking the answers through. From the prospect's point of view, you have behaved well every step of the way.

You have kept in touch before and after the meeting, you have come back with some well-thought-out recommendations within the promised time scale.

How many other people will they have met who behave in such a quality way? After all, quality service is only doing exactly what you say you will do within the time frame agreed on.

As I write about this step, I am reminded that I recently arranged two appointments through gatekeepers whom I had met, and to whom I had written a well-deserved note of thanks previously. In one case I had taken flowers as well. Without them it might have been six weeks before I could have arranged what I actually did accomplish in five minutes through them.

When I am dealing with a large number of assistants in an organisation, I draw a rough chart in my diary of where everyone sits, their names and who they report to. Then when I go in, I know which person does what and where I can find them.

Getting the spelling of their names right is very important. One that I spend time with is Karin, as opposed to the more usual spelling of Karen. If I were to get the spelling wrong on a thank-you note, it would really spoil my best efforts. Another instance: recently, after someone was very helpful, I wrote to thank him and later phoned to tell him the positive result of his introduction.

He commented that my letter was in his, 'Nice letter file, that had remarkably few in it.' I know that he does a great deal for people, so why so few 'thank-you' notes?

It takes but a few minutes, but is remembered forever.

'I think it would be a good idea.'
Mahatma Ghandi (1869–1948)
when asked what he thought of Western civilisation.

IDENTIFYING PEOPLE YOU KNOW BY THEIR PHONE STYLES

Talking their language is easy when you know how and what to look for. Make a first try at identifying prospects and clients by their personality types, using the information you have just read about telephone style and language. See if you can write in the name of at least one person after each of the following styles:

- Aspirer (entrepreneurial type)
- Enquirer (chief financial officer type)
- Admirer (human resources type)
- Inspirer (visionary, head of large corporation type)

SECRETS OF GOOD PHONING

'For people who like peace and quiet: a phoneless cord.'
Unknown

When you are feeling anxious, the tension can come through in your voice and create problems for you on the phone. Research shows that an anxious man sounds elderly, inflexible, irritable, bad-tempered. Tense women can be judged to be irrational, emotional and unstable.

You can get rid of tension before you phone, by relaxing your mind and your muscles. Take a deep breath, tighten up all over, clench your fists and toes, stretch your legs and hold for a slow count of five.

Relax and breathe out for a count of five. Take another deep breath, hold for a count of five, breathe out and relax. Make sure that your teeth are unclenched by putting your tongue against the back of your top front teeth.

Continue to breathe quietly: five seconds in, and five seconds out. Feel a deep, calm relaxation flowing through your whole body. Concentrate on your breathing—in for five, out for five. Soothe yourself by picturing yourself doing something relaxing that you love.

Above all else, when making your call, care about the person at the other end. Be polite and respectful. Always keep in mind the four types of professionals with whom you may be dealing. Avoid wasting the other person's time, or on the other hand, not spending enough time for the other individual to feel comfortable with you.

Staying in control

There are powerful ways of staying in control of a call. One way to sound more authoritative is to stand up while phoning. Your whole system will be more aroused and alert, your sense of power is heightened and your mind is sharpened. A smile will make you sound affirmative, bright and happy.

Smiling is a good tactic to use when you are talking to Aspirers, who can be intimidating by the rapidity and brusqueness of their speech. Conversely, not smiling can make you sound flat, dull and tired. Not at all a pleasure to talk to.

On the other hand, if you're after an appointment to sell a holiday in the sun and you want to sound relaxed and casual, there is no harm in lounging back in your chair and chatting with an Admirer or an Inspirer as though you were sitting on the beach.

Effective listening

Earlier we looked at design techniques and saw that it was important to position your copy either on the left—or right-hand side of the page in order to send the desired message to the reader. Similarly, it makes a difference whether you listen to a caller with your right ear or your left, believe it or not!

Listen with your right ear to evaluate complicated facts, because the right ear communicates with the cool, analytical left side of your brain.

'Experience teaches you to recognise a mistake when you have made it again.'
Unknown

Right-ear listening is helpful when you speak with an Aspirer or an Enquirer, to understand information correctly and respond logically.

To listen sympathetically, hold the phone to your left ear. This transmits information to the right side of your brain, the hemisphere of intuition, imagination and creativity. By increasing sensitivity to unspoken emotions, left-ear listening enhances empathy. Admirers and Inspirers generally listen with their left ears, and should be heard with your left ear, because they are attuned to emotions.

Do I use these techniques myself? Yes I do and I find it very useful for focusing on detail where necessary and for thinking creatively where necessary. I actively switch the phone over to the relevant ear, and yes, I do spend most of my time standing up and smiling for phone calls.

There are two main barriers to effective listening. The first is distraction: doing two complicated tasks at the same time, such as reading while you are taking a call.

Decide priorities. If the memo is more urgent, read it before you get on the phone. Otherwise, you will listen only to the first few words and then concentrate on the reading. The second barrier is dismissive listening, which occurs when someone has a problem and because we are not pleased with what we are hearing, we want to interrupt.

To avoid this, attend not only to the spoken words but also to those left unsaid. Say as little as possible while you are listening. Encourage the other person to continue.

Murmur phrases like 'I see', or 'I understand', or 'That's interesting', or 'Do tell me more'. Thus, the speaker feels welcome to speak freely.

Keep your feelings to yourself for the moment. Don't get angry and dismiss what the person is saying by responding too soon. Wait until you've heard everything; take notes, and pinpoint the critical issues.

Then come back calmly and quietly when you've both had a chance to get to the root of the problem. The right time to express your side of the argument is after you've listened long enough to understand the other person's problem exactly. Don't take the issue personally. You are only sorry about it; you didn't cause it.

As a case in point, my client, IMCOR in New York, upgraded their computers. After a few days' use, the computer crashed, causing a great deal of distress and loss of updated documents.

Among the losses were recent changes to my book, painstakingly marked up by my editor and keyed in by my assistant during some late nights at the office.

Unknowingly, I happily returned to my editor what I thought was the most recent version. Her phone call to me made it very clear that a great deal of her editing had not been done and she was justifiably upset.

Now in the old days I would have become defensive and upset, too. This time I just murmured along and agreed that it was an incredible waste of her time and hard work. Later I found out what had happened and we were able to discuss it amicably. I was sorry about it, but I didn't cause it.

A good aid to effective listening is to check your understanding by feeding back key points at suitable moments. Say, 'So you're suggesting that . . .', or 'Then we agree that . . .'. Checking important points prevents much wasted effort and encourages you to take good notes as the conversation proceeds. Head your notes with the date and time of the call and the caller's name, phone number, title and company. You have a record of what went on by doing no more than stapling your notes together and putting them into your file.

'If I had done everything that I'm credited with, I'd be speaking to you from a laboratory jar in Harvard.'
Frank Sinatra

Take time to write a letter or memo that confirms your understanding of the discussion and what you have both agreed to do next. Mail, fax or deliver it as soon as you can after the discussion. The longer you wait, the less the recipient trusts your notes as their memory has gone dim, too.

Do these tips and techniques really work?

Recently a friend of mine who teaches tele-sales had a student who had already won a tele-sales award. At lunch time the other students crowded around and asked how he had done it. 'I read a book and did what the author said,' he replied, but refused to name the book.

After much nagging he said that it was written by a woman.

My friend, Carolyn, picked up the scent and said, 'It was Wendy Evans, wasn't it?' and he reluctantly agreed.

When asked why he had not wanted to share the information, he said that he didn't want the rest of the world competing! Needless to say they promptly went out, bought my book, and did just that. Again, success is simple.

Saying goodbye is a true skill

We have all seen it: colleagues holding the phone at arm's length and making winding motions with their other arm. The person at the other end is just not going to hang up.

Being caught on the phone is a sign that you have lost control of the conversation. Ending your call efficiently is as important as starting it correctly.

Say goodbye in a way that builds the relationship

It is unlikely that you will ever get a long goodbye from Aspirers (the entrepreneur type), because they are in such a hurry to hang up. If you do want to say goodbye first, put the reason for ending the call firmly back into the other person's zone.

Say, 'Thank you for your time. I won't keep you any longer because I know you're busy.'

'Most of our future lies ahead.'
Denny Crum, American football coach

Bring a conversation with Enquirers (accountant types) to a suitable conclusion by promising to send them a fax or letter to confirm your conversation.

They are happy when they know the substance will be available in black and white. They can put it into the file and cover themselves against any possible problems.

Admirers (human resources types) hate to be cut short. They see it as a form of rejection. Don't sound as though it is goodbye forever. Say, 'It has been nice talking to you. Speak to you again soon.'

Inspirers (visionaries) are far less sensitive to hasty goodbyes. Being bored so easily, they always want to rush off to something new. Say something like 'I must dash,' and you will be talking their language.

When dealing with a relative stranger, be polite. Use the person's name in your final sentence, but be hesitant to use the first name unless you have been invited to do so. It is better to be thought of as very polite rather than too pushy and friendly.

Say, 'Thank you, Ms Jones, I will send you a fax,' or 'Thank you, Mr Smith, I will be in touch.'

If there is some information you particularly want remembered, repeat it immediately before saying goodbye. We often remember what people said at the beginning and at the end, but we may not recall what they said in the middle.

Do not be diverted into a difficult discussion. If someone wants information that you cannot give at present, such as more precise costs or details, say something like, 'I don't have that information at hand at present, but I shall find it and get back to you.'

Why are you making the call?

Always keep in mind the purpose of your call. Remember that your first phone call to an organisation is not to sell; you are only setting up an appointment. The first rule of cold calling is, 'Never sell over the phone.'

People will of course say, 'Why should I see you?' and instead of selling to them, use your single-minded proposition. If you worked for Minolta, for instance, you could use their previously mentioned statement: 'Because we understand the office.'

The listener's brain is going to do one of two things: he is either going to think that his office is perfect and he does not need you, or he will decide that his office could do with some help and an appointment might be a very good idea.

You are not selling on the first phone call; you are simply letting them decide whether they do or do not want to meet with you.

You have to build a relationship and identify needs before you can sell, so all you are seeking is an appointment to meet. That's all you want at this stage, just the opportunity to meet and identify the other's needs.

If you can help, after spending considered time on their issues and what it is that you have to offer, then you can start selling.

If the answer is 'no' to an appointment, thank them and remind them that you will be calling back within three months. (Remember 'no' means 'no, not now,' not 'no forever'.)

Recently I got a 'no' and was advised that the company had just taken on another consultant, whom they named. I accepted it at the time but then, knowing that we were complementary rather than similar in what we did, I rang back and re-pitched.

I got the appointment and the business. Later, when I was introduced to the team I was to train, the Managing Director stated that I was a living example of my philosophy that 'no' means 'no, not now', not 'no forever'. So be grateful for the 'no' answers.

Why? Because you couldn't handle appointments with all of your two hundred or so prospects at the same time, any-way—you would die from exhaustion! When they say 'yes', it will be because they do really want to see you.

Make cold calls work for you (have fun on the phone!)

First, let's address the subject of rejection.

As stated earlier, all over the world when I speak to groups, I ask, 'Put up your hands if you have ever had a second call from a salesperson to whom you first said no.' About 10 to 15 per cent of hands are raised. Then I ask, 'Keep your hands up if you have ever had a third call from a salesperson to whom you have firmly said no twice.' Virtually all hands go down.

Yet we know that it is in the fifth cycle of three-monthly (or less) call-backs that we really get the appointments.

'So what caused this fear of calling back?' I asked myself. I remembered as children that we never took no for an answer, we simply nagged until we got what we wanted—be it an ice-cream or a skateboard or whatever was the 'in' thing at the time.

We now call this the ice-cream theory.

You ask for an ice-cream and the answer is no. You nag and keep on nagging and 10 years later you have had a thousand ice-creams. So when did we start believing that no meant no forever? When did rejection start to hurt so much?

'Como frijoles?' (Spanish for 'How have you bean?') Unknown

Suddenly I thought back to my teenage years when I first found that no meant no forever. There I was all dressed up and excited at my first school dance. All dressed up and ready to dance with my first boyfriend, all night.

Only he danced all night with my girlfriend. For the first time I knew that no meant no forever. I knew the feeling of total rejection.

When I ask others if this has happened to them, everyone agrees that they had a similar experience and it too made them afraid of that word or attitude that says 'no'.

So now we know. In sales we have to revert to childhood, when 'no' was the signal to bide our time until it was 'yes'.

Now that we know why we fear rejection, let's accept that it is okay for people to say 'no, not now'. Let us set out to get some 'yes' answers by staying in touch, regularly and relentlessly, within 90 days or less, until we do.

Since good phone calls are great one-act plays, pace your delivery to match that of the person you are speaking to. Look for clues as to their personality style. Are they an Aspirer, Enquirer, Admirer, or Inspirer? Adapt to their style and make their day a happier one for having heard from you. Think back to when you were a child and knew instinctively what sort of mood the adults were in. You had only to walk into the room or hear their voices to know whether it was a good day or a bad one for them.

The same thing can be picked up on the phone, usually by the way in which people say hello. There may be a certain tightness in their voice. Regardless of whether you pick up that clue, always ask people at every level of the organisation if it is a good time for them to speak to you.

I usually say, 'Good morning, Paul, it's Wendy Evans speaking. Can you talk now, or have I caught you at a bad time?' If I know the person better: 'Hi Ros, it's Wendy. Is it okay for you to speak now?'

In my whole phone-answering life, only one person has ever consistently done that to me—and am I grateful! That person is Stephen Hickmore of 'The Search Advantage'. Stephen specialises in finding staff for the hospitality industry and has my undying respect for this simple courtesy. It reminds me to do it more often!

The reason is that not everyone has a gatekeeper and not every gatekeeper is at their desk when you phone. People can often be in a meeting in their offices when you ring. The simple courtesy of checking if it is convenient to speak now will always win you points.

You will readily be given another time to call back if you ask quickly but politely. You could say something like, 'Just give me a time that is convenient and I'll call back then.'

As I urged before, write notes as you talk and make sure that as details or decisions change during the conversation, you update the notes.

When you note an appointment in your diary, fill in all the details, including the address and phone number of the person and company you are going to see. Then if you are running late, you have one source that is always full of correct detail: your diary. A flip of the page and you can make that quick call to notify the person of the delay.

Saying thank you in a memorable way

As we said earlier, always write to thank everyone who has helped you: the person who sent you the company's annual report and promotional literature, the gatekeeper who helped you get the appointment, the person you met with and anyone else in the organisation who referred you.

'The brain is a wonderful organ; it starts working the moment you get up in the morning and does not stop until you get to the office.'
Robert Frost (1874–1963)

Tell those who were not at the meeting how it went, thank them, and if another action has resulted, write to tell them how that turned out. Think of how often you yourself have helped other people and the silence afterwards was deafening.

Vary your thanks. It is all too easy to send a typed note on company letterhead. All that is required is a signature, an envelope and a stamp. There must be many millions of these going around the world daily, achieving little in the way of impact.

You can make sure your 'thank you' will be remembered if you do it in a way that shows you really noticed the kindness and assistance received: you can send a handwritten note-card.

If you are not sure that your handwriting is easy to read, use a calligraphy felt tip pen instead. Practise the calligraphy strokes with the help of the instruction leaflet. The improvement will be extraordinary. The pens can be bought at any stationers. Blue looks better than black for thank-you notes.

Look around for memorable note-cards, the kind that are blank inside. You can find these at a bookstore or a museum or art gallery bookshop. Make sure they look so attractive that people will hesitate to throw them in the wastepaper basket.

I found some Japanese lacquer screen cards in black and gold at the Metropolitan Museum in New York. They cost no more than other quite ordinary cards but looked much more special. Even a year later, these cards were still on display in offices when I visited.

Keep a big box of your memorable cards close by. Try to choose cards that appeal to both men and women or have a box of each. Make sure the cards are congruent with the image of your company that you want people to receive. A few minutes and a few cards later, you will have added considerably to your clients' and prospects' memories of your meeting.

The moment you feel a 'thank you' is due, handwrite a

greeting card and send it off with your business card. It's like paying your bills. You get a wonderful feeling of: 'I've done it and it's out of the way.'

And remember that you can use this practice with prospects and clients when you have been unable to reach them by phone, just to say, 'Sorry I missed you, I'll be in touch within three months.'

Consider sending postcards to clients and warm prospects when you are away on business or on holidays. I send one to the client and one to the gatekeeper, with my contact details and the date of return.

They will already have been given the details to both, but a bright card has more impact and is easier to find than the original note. To prospects the message is more simple: 'I am away, but will be in contact when I get back.'

'I improve on misquotation.'
Cary Grant

Do you find it difficult to say 'thank you' in a way that shows genuine appreciation? It can be as difficult to say 'thank you' in a sincere way as it is to leave a message on an answering machine. Those of us who are usually competent with business language sometimes disintegrate when we have to write a card or leave a clear message on a machine.

Nevertheless, it is important to personalise your 'thank you', and it's not difficult to do if you use this simple technique:

> Set up a mental picture of the person you're going to contact and prepare a message as though that person were standing in front of you.

Now it will be easier for you to look at her or him and say or write, 'You were very kind and I appreciated your time and patience. Thank you for your help.' Or even, 'Thanks, you were great. Much appreciated.'

Use this technique every time you have to write, be it a thank-you card, letter, brochure, flyer, or a company's 'address to the nation'. By having a clear picture of that one person whom you most want to hear the message, you come across as a genuine person—which you are, as you are not trying to communicate with the whole world, just with that one important person.

Your style is your own, your message is for them and they feel it, hear it and see it as a real communication.

To back this up, I was fortunate to attend a Saatchi & Saatchi 'creative week' in Singapore, where much was achieved—including some work.

We asked one of the creative stars how he created a global campaign. Andy replied that he certainly did **not** try to put in a black cow, a white sheep, a brown dog. Or a redhead, a blonde and a brunette. Or even a man, a woman and a child.

He quite simply sat down to create something that was absolutely perfect for him. When he was satisfied, there was every chance that other people around the world would love it, too.

Ever since that workshop, I too have sat down to create for myself and just one other person, who represents the buyer. If I am writing about a product for a mother and baby, I get to know well just one mother and baby, and I write to them. Then there is every chance that other mothers and babies will hear me, too.

This way you shift the 'monkeys' off your back: the gibbering voices that call at you to please the boss, the client, the marketplace, your parents, your family, your friends. When these monkeys rule you, you please no one, not even yourself. Get rid of them and you please yourself and the world.

A further tip: never start a letter or card with the words

'Thank you', as when people see those opening words they think they have got the whole message.

By leaving the thanks until last, you force them to read all the words in case there are other things they ought to know. And there may well be, as you might be reconfirming a further appointment or providing them with some requested details.

MAKE NOTE-CARDS WORK FOR YOU

Think about the pleasure you get at Christmas and birthdays when you open the mailbox and find caring messages from people you like. Perhaps you can communicate with your clients in a way that makes it clear your response is meant for them as individuals. For example:

You're a doctor; you've just seen a new patient and prescribed a likely cure. Consider sending a 'get well' card and following up with a phone call to see how the patient is doing.

You're a travel agent whose customers are on their way back from a trip you arranged. Send a 'Welcome home' card and ask them to call and tell you about their experiences. If they do not phone you (being busy on their return, they probably won't), be sure to phone them.

You run a hotel and new clients were big spenders in the bars and restaurants. You can be fairly sure, by their joyous disregard for sleep or cost and their delight in having fun, that they are Inspirers. Inspirers love a 'thank you' and recognition.

So mail a 'Thank you for staying with us' card to their business address. Put a note inside and ask them to let you know when a return trip is planned, so that you can put a special gift in their rooms.

Give them three gift choices and arrange for their selection to be in their rooms before arrival. Upgrade them to a better room, if they have not already booked the most expensive

'If it weren't for the last minute, nothing would get done.'
Unknown

suite. You will more than get your money back in their expenditure in the restaurants and bars, as this personality type always returns a favour. Perhaps they will enjoy the experience so much that you will hear from their friends as well.

Why not send birthday cards to everyone who has ever stayed with you, as does the Peninsula Hotel in Hong Kong? For years I have heard about and seen these birthday cards. I now think it is probably the single most successful ongoing promotion I have come across, because it really suits a grand hotel to remember people in this way.

Birthday cards can apply to whatever industry you're in. If you're in insurance, send a birthday card on the date of the policy renewal; if you are selling cars or real estate, send a birthday card on the date the owner bought the car or house. This practice is fun and it makes you memorable.

Again, never delay sending your thanks. The closer your note is to the action, the more powerful the effect of a 'thank you' on the person who contributed.

Recently I received two personal notes, one to say 'thank you' for a lunch and the other from a dentist. Both were handwritten. The first was a very elegant card. The second was a note on company letterhead welcoming me to his practice. The card is up on the bookshelf; sadly the dentist's company letterhead is in the bin.

'It's fun being in the same decade as you.'
Franklin Delano Roosevelt in a letter to Winston Churchill, 1942

While I was enormously impressed that the dentist sent me a handwritten note, it is hard to put it anywhere but in the bin. Not so with the card. Grab the occasion to send cards that people will display and thus remember you constantly.

KEY POINTS TO REMEMBER

Look upon your phone calls to clients and prospects as one-act plays designed to give them pleasure, thereby benefiting you.

- Never sell on the first phone call; the first call is only to set up an appointment. Remember to use your single-minded proposition as to why they should give you the appointment.
- Always start with the head of any corporation with which you want to do business. You can get passed down an organisation but not up.
- Say 'thank you' in a memorable way. Always send a card when thanks are due. Use cards also to say, 'Sorry I missed you.' Use cards to invite, to remind, or just to say 'hi'. Make sure the card matches the corporate image you display and **always put in your business card.**

■ ■ ■

All over the world, people have said to me that they have contacted everyone once and have not liked to go back because they did not know what to say next. I had exactly the same experience when I represented the Peninsula Hotel Group Hong Kong as their regional sales manager in Australia.

I called on the whole of the travel industry, distributed brochures and price lists for the many Peninsula Group properties in Asia, got lots of commitment to using the hotels, and then nothing much happened!

The sales manager at Cathay Pacific (where I had my office) told me to go back and do the same thing all over again. I did, it worked and that is what I now recommend. Do the same thing over and over again until the message gets through. Growth Skill 7 will help you do that.

■ 'Personal satisfaction, I believe, must come from a day-to-day feeling that one has earned their pay.'
Leo Burnett

GROWTH SKILL 7
BE ABSOLUTELY CONSISTENT IN YOUR FOLLOW-UP

Of the hundreds, perhaps thousands of people who phone your prospects, you are probably the only one who is making contact every 90 days or less. You come across as serious and committed. You want the prospect's business, and you have proved it by staying in touch. They can't help but think that if you manage your business this well, imagine what you could do for them.

You may be wondering why, if it's as simple as consistent contact, everyone's business isn't growing by leaps and bounds. The fact is that most people think they have said everything after the first round of mailing and phoning, and they don't know what to do next. Often nothing further is done.

There is a tendency to think that the prospects will ring in when they need something. That doesn't very often happen!

The simple truth is that you must stay in contact and say the same thing the second, third, fourth and fifth time and ever after, but with minor variations.

'The future is much like the present, only longer.'
Don Quinsenberry

The good news is, as we have said, that 60 per cent of all sales opportunities arrive after the fifth contact. At about fifteen months of contacting in three-month cycles, appointments will begin to come in droves. When I returned to New York to follow up on IMCOR's success, they were on their fifth three-month cycle of contacting 8000 prospects

America-wide. As I arrived they said, 'Just as you promised, we are overwhelmed with success, exactly on the 15th month, and yes, we are having trouble keeping up!'

Mind you, I can be wrong. It can happen sooner—depending on the product, the promotion and the market demand.

Recently two women, who were friends, both left their jobs in insurance to become self-employed. They visited another friend, Maureen, and expressed their concern that although they had an idea, they didn't know how to get started.

Maureen had a copy of my book and said, 'Read this.' Which they did for two days and nights and then went into their secretarial placement and temping business.

When they saw Maureen next, they said, 'Tell Wendy Evans she is wrong. It doesn't take 15 months—we were in profit in the first month!' I don't mind being wrong for that kind of happy beginning.

In Australia, Thomas Cook had a busy office at the north end of Bankstown shopping centre. One day I analysed the postcodes of their clients and found they all came from the north; they drove into the shopping centre from that point, shopped at that end of the shopping centre and drove away.

If Thomas Cook had put in offices on the south, east and west sides they would have quadrupled their business.

The Mars Bar people found the same thing in New York. The city blocks are big enough to have multiple corner stores, and analysis showed that different outlets sold different sweets depending on the socio-economic standing of the people coming the quickest way down their streets for their supplies.

When you choose the business you want to be in, let it be a simple one to promote—regularly and relentlessly—within

'A company in which anyone is afraid to speak up, to differ, to be daring and original, is closing the coffin door on itself.'
Leo Burnett

90 days. People are complex and simple at the same time. The least amount of effort that they have to expend, mentally and physically, to make a decision to purchase, the more successful you will be.

Allow yourself to become as single-minded about your business as the Coca-Cola Company. Coca-Cola has spent billions on marketing and continues to do so. This giant international company consistently outlays a colossal amount ($500 million and more per annum in the United States alone) to sell its product, single-mindedly saying the same things over and over again, in what look like new and different ways.

SINGLE-MINDED REPETITION

The reason it's necessary to be single-minded is that our lives tie up about 99 per cent of our brains: work, home, finances, children, in-laws, weddings, divorces, medical issues, birthdays and holidays, bosses, cars—the list is endless.

Regular, single-minded contact with prospects is the only way to make them take notice of you. You may have found that your first round of mailing and phoning netted a one-half to one per cent response, with people actually saying 'Yes' to appointments and some even giving you business.

This suggests that your mailing package and phoning program were successful, so do not change anything significantly.

With the second round, there is the temptation to design something entirely new in order to excite yourself and everybody around you. Resist that temptation. You can design a variation on your original theme, but at all costs defend your right to bore yourself and your workplace associates.

Some examples: the little red man on the Johnnie Walker scotch bottles has never varied; the Christian Dior pink oval stands out on packs you have no idea about except that they are from Dior; the Mercedes star would say Mercedes no matter where you found it; roses will always stand for love and romance; diamonds have little more glitter than glass but the endless romantic advertising ensures that no wise man would ever give a piece of glass instead.

Yes, you can repeat yourself endlessly, as Coca-Cola does. When you think of straying from the path, ask yourself, 'Has Coca-Cola ever changed its image significantly?'

It has always been a fun product for lively beautiful people who go leaping around beaches and mountains and cities, in and out of surf and snow, up and down and around on roller blades and do wonderful, happy things while drinking Coke.

Coke refreshes!

If Coca-Cola's message hasn't changed significantly over the years, your own successful message need not change either. Continue to bore yourself; you won't be a bore to the outside world.

IF IT'S TRITE AND BORING, DO IT!

Your message may seem trite and boring to you because you are so close to your product. However, the rest of the world doesn't know about your great product story. When you have a clear idea of who you are, what your product is and what it has to offer, don't give up. Keep on offering it until your prospects notice it, too.

The first time you put your product message in a covering letter, say something like, 'May we introduce you to . . .?' The second time around, you can say, 'May we remind you that . . .?' The third time you could say, 'Again, may we call your attention to . . .?' The fourth time around try, 'We would like to remind you . . .'

'If you have a job without aggravations, you don't have a job.'
Malcolm Forbes

Never give up on your basic, central message. You are exactly who you are. Present your product or service continually and without much deviation. If you deviate, you may confuse that tiny bit of the 1 per cent that is listening to your message, and you will be the loser.

Make it easy for people to find you. Have your address and contact number big and bold. Pass your letterhead through your fax machine and make sure the numbers are still clear to read. Of all the faxes I get, about 10 per cent are readable in that area, as corporate ID designers still think people mail letters—when we know that we fax far faster and more effectively.

So stay with it. When you are yawning at the mere thought of ever saying the same thing again, when you are bored to tears with those words or pictures, that's when the outside world is beginning to listen to you.

> 'If you want a place in the sun, prepare to put up with a few blisters.'
> **Abigail Van Buren**

To a travel client we recommended selling Bali holidays on a 'Buy-one-get-one-free' basis. The travel agency groaned. They were sick to death of the sound of Bali. But all available travel statistics showed that the youth market was still very interested in travelling to Bali and was not in the slightest bit bored by the sound or sights of Bali.

'Go with the flow,' we said. 'You want to get young people inside the door, so capture them by offering what they want. When it is trite and boring to you, do it!' It worked. The travel company established a good base of young travellers and went on to sell them many other products in the youth holiday range.

Remember, repeat yourself until you are so sick with boredom that you wish your product or service had never been invented. Stay in touch with prospects in a positive and caring way, within the three-month cycle. Your only mission in your business life is to help people clearly understand what it is you offer so that they will buy from you in their own time.

Make being trite and boring work for you (yawn, sob!)

Have you repeated your central message to the point of being bored to tears in the past? Have you briefed your advertising agency to come back to you time and again with the same central message? Or did you cry out for something new and exciting and even move on to another agency to get a bright and vibrant new look?

If you did you are not the only one. In America alone, around 80 per cent of all clients move from one advertising agency to another within five years, probably for this very reason. It takes about two years to get a new advertising agency settled into the culture of the company they are trying to work with, and yet the first cracks of the honeymoon period are evident within 18 months. Another move is imminent.

It is no wonder that the public ignores so much of what is thrown at it. The ads are being prepared by people who know in their heart of hearts that no matter what they do, the next advertising manager in the job will call for five or six or even 40 agencies to come up with something bright and new; the account will move and they will be out of a job, again.

I had an advertising manager from a major company tell me that the first thing he does is move the business to show who is in charge. But not for long. Given a few months or years, he himself will move on, for whatever reason, and it will all start again.

Defend your right to be boring, but boring only to yourself. Get out everything that the public sees from your company and lay this enormous bundle on the boardroom table. Look for that central message, style, colour, layout, theme, feeling.

'Some people say three is the magic number and others say it's seven. But I'm here to tell you, Oliver, the only magic number is one.'
Fagin to Oliver Twist

Look for anything that makes you think the outside world has a chance of recognising your product message, be it on radio, TV, buses, billboards, newspapers, magazines or even match box covers!

Look for that continuity in your letters, brochures, flyers, instruction manuals. If you see a boring sameness, congratulations! If you do not, don't change your agency, just work with the one you have, to make it happen.

PERSISTENCE PAYS

There is another very important step in this quest for winning new business, that of persistence. Almost anyone can put these steps into place, but not many people will keep on keeping on for days, weeks, months, years afterwards. Nothing replaces persistence. Persistence is what makes the other steps so powerful.

Perhaps it seems a formidable task to put our new-business system into place and it may be so at the beginning. However, the advantage of persistently staying in touch within 90 days is that you incorporate into your daily operations a system for bringing you continual new-business opportunities.

The expenditures for the process are the costs of your written materials, your telephone, and the time spent by your staff. The first mailing campaign may cost between three and five dollars per prospective client, depending on the size and quality of your initial mailing package.

'Thank you for sending me a copy of your book. I will waste no time reading it.'
Moses Hada (1900–1966) in a letter

The second and subsequent mailings can cost less or more, depending on your budget and your planned scale of inclusions. The commitment in time is a minimum of two years (in three-monthly cycles), a fairly standard time period given that the average closing-the-sale cycle is between 15 and 18 months.

In financial services, for instance, Shearson Lehman confirmed a statistic that I have also noted during my consulting years: it takes around one hundred enquiries to convert into five pieces of business over a period of about a year. I found the same statistic true of executive recruiting in London.

We had to visit 100 companies before we found five really live possibilities, that is, companies that were unhappy enough with their current supplier to be prepared to move on.

Even then, it took a year to 18 months to get them settled into our organisation and get us up to handling them speedily and well. New business takes time.

Friend and mentor Willem Sprokkreeff was with the Hilton Hotel Group for many years and earned himself an awesome reputation for almost single-handedly dragging Australia's hospitality industry into total quality.

After 35 years of Hilton commitment, he retired and began consulting. In a recent meeting with him he said that he had found that it took $2 million worth of promises to get $200,000 worth of business. It is not easy!

The sad thing is, so many salespeople think they are failures because they cannot close the sale instantly. About the only thing you can sell instantly is food and drink to a hungry and thirsty person at the only oasis in the desert!

For the rest of us, it takes time, especially when the ticket item is high. I have heard it estimated that replacing demoralised sales staff each year is a six billion dollar industry. Salespeople are hounded by management to close **now**, and because it does not happen that way, they become discouraged, and they either resign or are retrenched.

As my friend Michael Hewitt-Gleeson points out, even with his offer of a reward of $10,000 for so doing, no one can prove that there is any part of the human brain which can be

> 'When it is not necessary to make a decision, it is necessary not to make a decision.'
> **Lord Falkland (1610–1643)**

manipulated into buying, until such time as that person has established a desire to do so. (Usually they then justify the purchase through greed, fear and laziness, but they have to like it first.)

The mailing and phoning program for developing new business is a cost-effective, relationship-building marketing tool that lets you track the expenditures and the benefits on a day-by-day, week-by-week, month-by-month basis. It is a technique that can benefit almost any size or type of business or service company.

You choose the clients you want in your business life and build trusting relationships with them, which lie at the heart of all business. The sale will follow.

Mailing and phoning around two hundred people over a three-month (60 working days) period means only a very few mailings and follow-up phone calls per day.

Never mail a huge amount all at once as you will get so far behind in trying to contact people for an appointment that you will be overwhelmed and will stop trying. Instead, mail three or four each night and after an interval of about a week, phone those three or four people.

If you don't reach them on the first try, try once more that day. If you reach them, terrific! If you don't, send a note-card saying 'Sorry I missed you. I will be in touch again within 90 days' and enclose your business card.

Keep going. Do not get bogged down in worrying about the two hundred or so people as a whole. Simply see them as three or four lots of mailings and a few phone calls per day.

Whether used together with other marketing strategies, or on its own, this program can be managed by an individual entrepreneur or by the secretary or assistant to the chief executive officer of a large company.

By making relationship-building with prospects a regular part of your business activities, not a once-a-year sales effort, you will always be in the middle of new-business building, whether times are good or bad. It is my belief that this is just the right solution for the present (and future!) unpredictable climate.

KEY POINTS TO REMEMBER

- Be persistent: contact within 90 days or less, but never more. Most people do not make even one business development phone call a day, regularly and relentlessly. They don't work through as little as 60 likely prospects over a three-month period.

- It can be that easy: as low as one prospect a day will generate rewards. Three a day is fine, five a day is excellent, because multiplied by 60 working days in three months, you will have 300 people you are phoning, sending cards to, faxing, following up on, sending articles to over a three-month period. And getting in lots of rewarding new business deals.

'I like work; it fascinates me. I can sit and look at it for hours.'
Jerome K. Jerome (1859–1927)

■ ■ ■

Next: Growth Skills 8 on sales promotion will help you close the sale by making a special offer to bring forward the purchase decision, in your favour.

GROWTH SKILL 8

SALES PROMOTION

We have said that people buy from greed, fear and laziness, once they have seen something they like. Well, this chapter is about touching the greed button, and more.

Consider this scenario:

You have provided dynamic written materials, you have had a successful appointment, the potential client seems pleased by what you have to offer. Still, they are wavering about giving you the business.

As always, you realise that you have hungry competitors wanting the business, too. In this case, a special offer on your part can make the difference. It says, 'I really want your business.' And gives the prospect a reason to stop thinking and start acting.

'Every time
a friend succeeds, I die
a little.'
Gore Vidal

The essence of sales promotion is that it must be easily understood by the client or prospect and relevant to your product. It will seem ludicrous to consumers to get a free embroidery kit if they are buying a puppy!

However, in hairdressing, for instance, you can promote your business using hairdressing products. In fashion, you can promote using accessories or perfumes. With books you can offer membership in a book club. Your offer has always to sound right and be related in some way to your product or service.

PROMOTIONAL TECHNIQUES

Here are a few types of special offers you can consider; they represent some of the best promotional vehicles I've seen in the past few years—with the exception of competitions, which I have included for discussion only.

A free gift with purchase

This is probably the most successful and affordable sales promotion on earth.

A high-quality gift lives on in the memory as a favourable experience of dealing with your company. My client Thomas Cook, as a free gift with purchase, gave away a beautiful leather travel wallet with separate pockets for all the paperwork, passports, tickets, money, travellers cheques, etc, that travellers need to carry.

Made of the finest leather and very well constructed, these wallets look good fifteen years later and are an ongoing quality testimonial for Thomas Cook. I still use mine and am delighted every time I line up at the check-in counter to have such a useful and attractive item. The offer also brought the company a great amount of business at the time.

If you really want to move your product, think of offering a free gift with the purchase of a certain dollar amount of merchandise or services: a free sunroof when you buy a car; free shirts or ties with a suit; free software with a computer; an extra month's free advertising space with a six-month campaign; free shampoo and conditioner with a hair colour treatment.

'Logic is in the eye of the logician.'
Gloria Steinem

Buy one, get one free

Buy a suit or dress and you will receive another free. Have your eyes examined and another family member's examination is free. This can also be expressed as two for the price of one, or 50 per cent off.

Of the three possible ways of expressing this offer, the 'buy-one-get-one-free' statement is stronger than 'two for the price of one' or '50 per cent off'. The first phrase contains the word 'free', which is one of the most powerful words in the English language.

Buy two (or more) and get one free is also powerful, depending on the price of the purchased item. For instance, buy eight motor cars and get one free would be a great offer to a company buying a fleet and it would be more impressively conveyed than would be: '12 per cent off the price of each of the eight cars'.

The Peninsula Hotel in Hong Kong buys Rolls Royces in large numbers and I have often wondered what sort of an offer Rolls Royce makes . . .

Imagine the advertising: 'Buy seven Rolls Royces, get one free.' It is, after all, a discount of only an eighth. The only trouble with Rolls Royces is that the luggage-carrying capacity is small and when major players in the clothes stakes came to town, such as Imelda Marcos, the Peninsula Hotel had to send out several trucks to bring in her luggage.

'If it were not for Philo T. Farsworth, inventor of television, we'd still be eating frozen radio dinners.'
Johnny Carson

A banded offer

This involves putting two things together with a band around them.

When you sell four litres of paint banded with a half-litre of turpentine, make the banded price somewhat less than the price of both if sold separately.

You have now created a promotion worthy of attention and you will sell more of each item than ever before. A toothbrush with toothpaste or mouthwash is a good banded offer; so is pantihose with a second pair, detergent with fabric softener, and deodorant with talcum powder. These kinds of offers work very well.

Price reductions

This technique will get customers flocking in, but use such sales discreetly, so that you have no more than two per year.

You don't want to appear to be buying your way out of trouble. When you have this type of sale, make it such a terrific value that people line up for your product. Those who buy merchandise at your sales once or twice and are treated well may develop loyalty to your business and come back again outside of the sales season.

> 'I believe that the power to make money is a gift from God.'
> **John D. Rockefeller (1839–1937)**

It seems that the stores with the best sales also allow you to return the sales goods for a full refund. Clients will say, 'And they even gave me all my money back, without any argument.' The less significant companies usually have a no-returns policy. Which would you shop at in the future?

Sampling

A small sample of the product is delivered to your home. Many years ago a new soap powder appeared in my letter box, and when used, refused to dissolve in any temperature of water. It just swirled around in little pellets with the washing.

Apart from arousing my wrath, the sample achieved nothing except my refusal to ever buy the product. However, where the product is a good one, it can encourage purchase when the first use has proven its worth.

Vouchers and coupons

These arrive in your home as inserts in newspapers or magazines or in household letter box drops.

They offer you money off the company's product to encourage purchase and trial use. After that it is over to the shopper to decide whether the item is bought again.

Quality service

This can be the best sales promotion technique!

The Regent Hotels have a service policy which goes so far beyond the norm that guests can't help but comment, 'And they even . . .!'

This is a brilliant promotion in itself. Whereas unhappy clients never stop telling people about how badly they were treated, happy clients barely murmur, unless it is an amazing case of 'And they even . . .!' If you are going to be talked about, let it be in the latter way.

Simple things, too, such as taking care of people's parcels is a kind gesture and a security measure. In New York you have to hand in any bag bigger than a small handbag, and even though it is an anti-theft process, it allows you to shop hands-free.

Recently in a well-respected department store, I tried to check in my overnight bag and was advised quite firmly that it was against security regulations. I could not carry it and shop at the same time, so I left.

In this case 'they even' made it seem a federal offence for me to have asked! I just do not feel like going back, despite having shopped there for many years.

Collector's items

'Buy old masters. They bring better prices than young mistresses.'
Lord Beaverbrook (1879–1964)

KLM Royal Dutch Airlines ran an excellent promotion offering everybody who flew first class a porcelain miniature of a Dutch house filled with liqueur.

People bought first-class tickets as never before so they could display these collectibles on their desks and show that they were high-class travellers of the world. If the collectible item you have in mind has a 'certain something', go for it, but test its appeal beforehand.

In fact, test every promotional offer of any kind before going all the way.

You can save yourself a lot of time and money if you test first and then fine tune it if it seems to be working. 'Doing something small in the corner first' is a very good technique for instituting any form of change more broadly across an organisation.

If you impose a major change on an organisation, it usually fails from fear, ignorance and confusion. But if you do a test first and it works well, the whole organisation hears of it and may well want it. (And if it fails, well, it was only a test after all.)

As mentioned elsewhere in this book, the human brain reacts to a new idea the way the human body does to a foreign protein: it rejects it. Hence doing something quietly and successfully in the corner first allows the other decision-makers in the organisation to bet on a good thing—and no doubt be promoted for so doing!

'How little you know about the age you live in if you think that honey is sweeter than cash in hand.'
Ovid
(43 B.C.–A.D.18)

The personality presenter: someone with name recognition endorses your product

However, celebrity endorsements have pitfalls. The endorser has to be totally believable, or the whole promotion becomes memorable for its failure.

So in general, avoid paying some powerful 'name' to endorse your product unless it is the equivalent of Florence Nightingale for bandages, Arnold Schwarzenegger for a fitness campaign, or Greg Norman for golf!

Competitions

In any competition, there must be some element of skill, such as writing a poem about why you would like to fly British Airways to London, with the winner getting a return trip for two.

There can be complex state laws governing competitions. Moreover, competitions are not as successful as other techniques in promoting sales because people never really believe they are going to win.

For the time and effort involved in putting together prizes for a competition, it would be much better to make a 'free gift with purchase' offer or a 'buy-one-get-one-free' offer. In many instances, a retailer can get free gifts from the suppliers of the product, so the end result is perhaps no more expensive than the competition process, but far more effective.

Remember, when you are working to close the sale with a prospect, consider promotional offers and how you can adjust some of these to suit your particular situation.

If you are in the service industry, try giving a discount when the account is pre-paid or paid within five working days. This can work so well that you may find you have fewer bad debts.

One of my clients paid an art studio within five days in order to get a 5 per cent reduction, while letting other companies that did not offer a discount wait 90 to 120 days!

In Singapore a hotel decided to offer a flat rate but got so many complaints from their local client companies that they marked the room rates up again and then gave back the expected fifteen per cent deduction. The end result was exactly the same, but saved 'face'.

Similarly, if you are in the consulting industry and do not wish to discount your fees, simply charge a little more and then offer a discount if paid in a period of time that suits you, such as five working days. If the bill is not paid within that time, you are owed the extra.

If yours is a product, probe for the prospect's needs and make your offer accordingly. Some examples include: free lawn mowing for a year if they hire you to landscape their garden, a garden umbrella if they buy a particular type of garden furniture, an extra twelve bottles of wine with the purchase of ten cases.

Once I met a man at a car dealership showroom who told me he had bought his previous car because they were giving away a free milkshake machine. He had two children, so thought it a good idea.

A friend in the travel industry offered a free cruise as an incentive to buy his house.

'To travel is to discover what is wrong about other countries.'
Aldous Huxley (1894–1963)

You may have seen a suburb at standstill because the local council was giving away free trees and an area in total chaos because the local greengrocer was selling two cabbages for the price of one. It happens!

You need not go that far. Instead you may wish to use a standard gift such as charity chocolates or peppermints. You could buy them outright and then offer them to your clients and customers as they leave.

This little gift works just as well in a professional services organisation as it does at retail level. People are people, and because they get tired and dry, a 'good cause' peppermint or tasty piece of chocolate is a great pick-me-up. It also creates an affectionate memory.

All things being equal, people do business with people they like and trust, and all things being unequal, they still do business with people they like and trust. Even the smallest of gifts makes you memorable.

When people see something they like, they justify the purchase through greed, fear and laziness. Be sure you touch the greed button, plus the others if possible, and the sale may well be yours.

MANAGING YOUR PROMOTIONS

The reality of good promotional activities is that they take time. You can't just leap out of bed and decide to have an 80-per-cent-off sale when you get to work.

Planning four to six months in advance is about right. That way you can do a little each day, and have your Mothers' Day promotion, for instance, happen comfortably, with time to spare to fix up the bits you may forget, such as the window notices or the envelopes to be ordered, or the mailing to your best customers for a preview day.

If you do a little each day, it does not break up your normal working day too much and adds another interest to your life.

'It is apparent that the company can't be any better or bigger than the growth of the people in it.'
Leo Burnett

Why not use the Saatchi & Saatchi three-month cycle for promotional activities?

You could plan to have four similar promotions to your client and prospect base each year. Your planning processes would become almost repetitive and therefore much easier to do.

Remember the principle of saying and doing the same things all the time, so that the public finally gets to notice you? For instance, in the service industry you could have four open days a year, or four half-day workshops with leading gods of industry. As a retailer you could have four 'free-gift-with-purchase' promotions; or four 'extra-product-free' weeks.

Planning several promotions over a year means making up a calendar of all the actions that have to be done in chronological order and sticking to it. If you are a retailer, for instance, wanting to promote Valentine's Day, Easter, Mother's Day, Father's Day, Christmas and New Year, you should be thinking and acting on those activities every day of your working life.

The skill is to find a simple, effective promotion that works for you and will only need tweaking to adapt it to all occasions. This is a great timesaver and it has the advantage of bringing a consistent look and sound to your advertising, point of sale and direct marketing communications.

Make sales promotion techniques work for you

Buy some women's magazines and notice all the sales promotion activities within their covers. Try to understand why the advertisers would make these offers; read all the fine print to see just how complex an operation a competition can be, for instance. When you plan to do sales promotion, remember these key issues:

'Veni, vidi, Visa' ('We came, we saw, we went shopping')
Jan Barrett

Keep it relevant to the objectives, to the product and to the needs of the customer/client or prospect.

Keep it simple. No one ever went broke underestimating the amount of time available to the consumer or client. We are all too busy to work our way through complicated offers, and your competitor may be offering a simple alternative. Winning a sale can be as easy as keeping it simple.

Keep it quality

Do nothing cheap; do everything well.

In the end quality service is the best offer of all. It is simply doing what you say you will do, within the time stated.

The good and the bad live on forever after the promotion. If you give shoddy goods, you will be shunned; if you give quality goods, you will establish an immediate rapport of respect between you and the client/prospect.

We look now at using special offers in contract negotiations to build an ongoing successful relationship with your new client.

THE CONTRACT IS STILL TO BE SIGNED

Why a contract? Because you want to get paid! There is no point in getting into a relationship where money is involved and then finding you have done all the work for no money or no proof that the money was owed.

This is especially important if you work as an agent and commission is owed to you; it could be conveniently forgotten if you don't get it down on paper.

While the prospect has identified a need for your product or service and you have made a relevant special offer, you may still find yourself without a signed contract. Think through again what you've done and what is left to do, to make that contract materialise.

Perhaps you thought that you and your prospect had come to an agreement about a contract, only to find that your prospect's thoughts were not in alignment with yours. There's always that moment when you return from a meeting thinking that it's all falling into place, but then something happens that is called 'post-purchase dissonance': everything seems to fall apart and you're completely unprepared for it.

Here are some issues to watch out for during your negotiations with a prospect:

1. Always remember that after they see something they like, people buy from greed, fear and laziness. Can you touch some or all of those buttons?

2. Be aware that there's often more to come after you've reached a verbal agreement with a potential client. A verbal agreement is usually a general understanding; a

written contract requires attention to detail and considerable compromise to get everything down and agreed to in black and white.

3. Get into the habit of agreeing on the little things before tackling the big ones. Strive for good and fair solutions.

4. Be considerate and flexible with the client or customer, remembering that a contract is not a legal document until signed. You don't want to scare people away by behaving as if your contract is ironclad when in fact you are willing to make concessions.

   Perhaps the prospect has already conceded something elsewhere, or it's an unusually large order, or the profits resulting from the contract will be very high. Be thoughtful of the client and your future. Do not kill the golden goose.

5. Let the client know that you intend the negotiations to be friendly and to result in a contract that both parties are happy to be entering.

   One of the problems with contracts is that people tend to consider the draft wording to be carved in stone. Not so; every word can be changed up to and including signing, providing both parties agree with the changes. But don't make changes just for the sake of doing so.

6. Describe your pricing so that it's easily understood: this is what it costs and why. Avoid subclauses and penalty clauses that make clients feel they are being punished if they do something the slightest bit different.

7. Check that your contract is relevant and readable. Don't rehash an old contract. Make sure it sounds as if it were written especially for this particular client. In addition, your contract will be easier to sign if its language is plain English. When a muddled contract document itself

'I may have my faults, but being wrong isn't one of them.'
Jimmy Hoffa (1913–1975)

becomes an issue, you're likely to find yourself facing costly delays in getting started.

8. Consider putting a clause into the contract that offers a discount on the cost of your product or service or a significant and relevant free gift if the agreement is signed by a certain date. When the offer is worthwhile, this can work wonders in getting the agreement through the various levels of approval.

9. Be aware that the only good negotiation is one in which both sides believe they have won a little. Think how great you feel when you come away from a discussion that led to what you wanted. It's even better when both sides feel that way.

10. Recognise that the contract you sign today may need to be altered in the future because your needs, or the client's needs, may change. How you react to a client's changed circumstances will impact on future contracts with the company and on referrals. Maintain a long-term view, be flexible and be sure that the new negotiations benefit both sides.

'It is better to be a mouse in a cat's mouth than a man in a lawyer's hands.'
Spanish proverb

The point made in the preceding paragraph is so important that I will reiterate it: closing the sale is often not closing the sale at all, it's just the beginning of many such interactions. Of course, once a contract is signed, you can foolishly demand that clients stick to the letter of the agreement, in spite of their changed needs.

However, if you insist on taking such an inflexible position, you might get through the term of that one contract (or fight it out in the courts) but there are not likely to be further contracts.

That kind of an attitude doesn't add up to long-term business. Be adaptable; you want to win for today and you also want to win for tomorrow. Try not to win the battle and lose the war. Rather, let both you and the client win, for future peace and prosperity.

In other words, be fair and friendly in your contract negotiations with your clients.

- Back to the files for some contracts. Get out any that you have been required to sign. Now ask yourself these questions:
- Did I understand exactly what I was getting into?
- Did I feel closer to the other person because of the signing of the contract?
- Was it laid out in an easy-to-read, plain English style?
- Was the tone warm and friendly?
- Would I look forward to another contract negotiation with this person/company?
- Did I feel fairly and intelligently treated?
- Was the layout of the contract well done, the quality of the paper good, the overall feeling one of importance, respect and dignity?

Now get out some contracts that you and/or your lawyers have drawn up for clients and customers to sign. Stand in the shoes of the client and ask the same questions as above. If you are not delighted with the answers, see if you can reword and redesign future contracts to change some of the not-so-good elements.

'Lawyers, I suppose, were children once.'
Charles Lamb (1775–1834)

KEY POINTS TO REMEMBER

- People buy from greed, fear and laziness, when they see something they like. Make relevant special offers to bring forward the purchase decision in your favour. 'Free gift with purchase' is probably the strongest, with 'buy one, get one free' and 'two for the price of one' a close second.

- When you get to the contract stage, draft a communication that totally focuses on the client from their point of view. Stress that every word is changeable until a mutually satisfactory agreement is reached. Make a special offer, valid until a reasonable date, to encourage them to get all the signatures on the document by that time.

- Use this stage to establish good working relationships. Start off in the spirit of harmony that will become the springboard for all future negotiations.

■ ■ ■

'Honesty is the best image.'
Ziggy (Tom Wilson)

So much to do, so little time. Growth Skill 9, on self-management of time and meetings as well as many other activities, will help you get the most out of your working and personal life.

GROWTH SKILL 9
HOW TO KEEP YOURSELF ORGANISED

MANAGE YOUR TIME SIMPLY AND EFFECTIVELY

G et rid of the unimportant things first so that they never become important, do the urgent and important things next and then let the other things interrupt—this is the dream I have for my day.

Up to the 'urgent' point I seem to be in control, but after that I am all too often overridden by other people's needs. So how can I (and we) change the effect that 'urgent' has on us?

First of all, we need to know what our objectives are, not only every day for the day, but also for the week, the month, the year and beyond. Be effective and efficient, but effective first and foremost. Our business and promotional plans, our strategic purpose are what give us control over other people's interruptive techniques.

'I never travel without my diary. One should always have something sensational to read.'
Oscar Wilde (1854–1900)

We have all experienced the telephone call that comes at the critical moment of a discussion; the staff member who urgently needs our help to finish a job not attended to until too late; the manager or associate who walks in the door and demands a meeting, now.

What do we do? Too often we respond, react and overreact to these pressures from people and things. We answer the phone, help the laziest member of the team and go off to the meeting unprepared and unwilling. There goes the day, blown as usual.

If, however, our working days were measured by the agreed business and promotional objectives that we had jointly set and which we reviewed and revised constantly, how might we have managed instead?

The phone could have been put on hold (either through an answering machine or a staff member). A specific time could have been allocated to help and review the performance of that lazy staff member. A rational explanation could have been given re the meeting: the job you were working on was urgent and important, but you would be free after 4.30 p.m.

All these power responses are relative to the objectives that were commonly agreed as being important for that day, that week, or longer. You take control by choosing time scales within which you can operate effectively and efficiently. Consider taking specific periods of time for the important issues.

Try 60 minutes of privacy for yourself, then open up for messages and be available for the next 30 minutes to respond to staff and management needs and return phone calls. Then close down for another 60 minutes, and open once more for 30.

I suggest trying a 60-minute cycle to begin with, because that is the recommended changeover time for driving long distances. Have you tried driving that way? If so, did you look forward to the changeover both ways?

'Never put off until tomorrow what you can do the day after tomorrow.'
Mark Twain
(1835–1910)

Perhaps you found at first you wanted to rest and watch the scenery, and next you wanted to drive and get on with it. Similarly, you might enjoy shutting down for an hour of private time, knowing that you are going to have a cup of coffee and get in touch with the world again shortly.

Alternatively, I met an executive who now takes and returns phone calls only between 3 p.m. and 5.30 p.m. After only three weeks of this regime, almost everyone now calls him between those hours.

They had learned two things: one, that he was not available until that time and two, that he always returned calls on the day, as promised. No hassles, no problems; people simply adapted to what they saw as a very fair, effective and efficient process.

The answer to time management, I suggest, is to know what your objectives are and stick to achieving them. Ensure that the balance is in your favour by allocating only as much time as you can truly spare to the interruptions and plagues of the day.

Either computerise your follow-up activities or use a tickler box (divided into month, week, days) to remind you of the follow-up calls that you promised to make—and will be remembered forever for so doing! And delegate, delegate, delegate.

MANAGING MEETINGS

All too often meetings end up going round and round the same subjects, everyone putting in their bit, little being resolved. Simon & Schuster in America required that no problem was to come to a meeting unless the following analysis had been written up and distributed beforehand:

PROBLEM-SOLVING MODEL

This exercise requires the participation of a subject and a practitioner. Or you can do it on your own if there is no one you can ask to talk it through with you.

Step A.
A identifies in a few words a problem currently being experienced.

Step B:
B asks A the following set of questions and writes down the responses.

1. What caused the problem?

_____

_____

_____

PROBLEM-SOLVING MODEL

2. How is this limiting you?

    _____

    _____

    _____

3. What are the long-term consequences of this situation if it continues?

    _____

    _____

    _____

4. Is this a recurring problem?

    _____

    _____

    _____

Step C:

B now asks A the following set of questions and writes in the responses.

1. What are three possible solutions?

    a _____

    b _____

    c _____

2. Which of these do you prefer?

    _____

    _____

    _____

3. What will that do for you?

    _____

    _____

    _____

4. How can you make it happen for you?

    _____

    _____

    _____

Often the problem never gets to the meeting, because the person owning the problem solves it by doing this work first.

EVALUATION

Here is an evaluation for use after meetings to find out how you can improve the next one.

- Why was the meeting called?

  _____

  _____

- Was the meeting really necessary?

  _____

  _____

- Was the purpose of the meeting met?

  _____

  _____

- Was the time convenient and the place suitable?

  _____

  _____

- Was the time limit met, and was it realistic to begin with?

  _____

  _____

- Did the agenda need to be sent out in advance? If so, was it?

  _____

  _____

- Should all participants have had input into the agenda? If so, did they?

  _____

  _____

EVALUATION

- Were supporting documents needed? If so, were they distributed?

  _____

  _____

- Did participants read and study them prior to the meeting, if asked to do so?

  _____

  _____

- Did the discussions remain relevant through self-management or through constant reminder?

  _____

  _____

- Did the participants stay with the agenda?

  _____

  _____

- Did all relevant people participate in the discussions?

  _____

  _____

- Were accurate records kept and effective minutes distributed within forty-eight hours?

  _____

  _____

- Are follow-up issues likely to be attended to? Or ignored until pursued?

  _____

  _____

- In the opinion of the group, was everyone there that needed to be?

  _____

  _____

EVALUATION

- Again, in the opinion of the group, was anyone there that should not have been?

  _____

  _____

- How satisfied was the group with the meeting?

  _____

  _____

- According to those who attended, what changes should be made?

  _____

  _____

- If you controlled this meeting, how would you do it better next time?

  _____

  _____

Does this questionnaire work?

Yes indeed. I used it with a client whose offices I had visited for a major meeting, which turned out to be a disaster. The interruptions exceeded the time given to their pressing problems, and I had a return plane journey to consider the best way to handle the problem.

That night I faxed them the above analysis. In response to the last question they stated that they would fly to my office instead. Which they did and, apart from the odd fax to my number for them, the meeting was totally focused.

So consider using this format for your own meetings until you refine them to the point of absolute usefulness and focus.

Here's another example: Recently I took a group of sales executives through this questionnaire process, based on their meeting with a prospect. We realised two things:

One: from the question, 'How satisfied was the group with the meeting?' that they had underestimated the importance of the Japanese process of enrolling all levels of the decision-makers and influencers: from top to bottom, centre left to centre right ('figure of eight'), informing everyone.

Hence they were getting blockades at different levels within the prospect's decision-making group.

Two: from the question, 'Are follow-up issues likely to be attended to? Or ignored until pursued?' it appeared that sales-people's follow-up left something to be desired because they feared the answer 'No'. It was easier not to phone and check whether or not they had the business, rather than risk rejection. They also lacked a closing technique because their product (in-house catering) was not urgent. As long as people were eating, changing to a better, more healthy and cost-efficient process was not important.

We workshopped the problem based on the philosophy that people buy from greed, fear and laziness. What offer could the company make that would bring forward the purchase decision? We thought that a fixed management fee for 18 months (if the decision was made in the next two months) would be a strong motivator, and the results were excellent.

Using the meeting analysis form can open up whole new ways of thinking and far more business. Try it!

Child, adolescent, adult, old age

It is important to remember that all meetings go through the following phases: child, adolescent, adult, old age. At first, people are nervous and irritable, thinking things like, 'Why am I here? Why can't they simply write a memo and let me get on with my work?'

'A stitch in time would have confused Einstein.'
Unknown

Then the adolescent phase kicks in: they drop their papers, fight for where they are going to sit, jostle for the milk and the biscuits, tell this week's funny stories.

At the adult stage, they decide that if they buckle down and get on with it, they may get out in time to sign the mail and go home.

Then old age kicks in: members get tired and crotchety and won't 'play' any longer. The key issue is to listen to their language during the adult phase and never to respond to their old-age comments.

In the adult phase they express interest, ask for more information, make positive remarks. In the old-age phase, they say things like 'We will call you when we are ready to proceed'; 'We will let you know when the budgets come through'; 'Don't call us, we will call you'. Ignore this. Remember the positive words in the adult phase and respond accordingly.

In America I met a woman who did not have meetings, she had 'deli-days'. She copied the process used by busy food counters: take a number and wait to be called. On her deli-days, staff took a number and waited for their turn to discuss their problems and issues with her. Keen staff got in early to get the earliest numbers. Each person was given as much time as they needed.

'Nothing is illegal if a hundred businessmen decide to do it.'
Andrew Young

SOME TIME MANAGEMENT ISSUES

Why not try colour-coded folders for managing your time:

- Important and urgent (red)
- Important, not urgent (blue)
- Not important but can appear urgent (green)

Stephen Covey, the author of **The 7 Habits of Highly Effective People**, has a matrix on time management issues. His four quadrants are as follows:

1. Important and urgent: crises, pressing problems, deadline-driven projects. Consider having a large red file for this.

2. Important, not urgent: preparation, *new-business activities, crisis prevention, values clarification, planning, relationship-building, true recreation. Consider having a large blue file for this. (*Though I believe that new business activities should be in 'Important and Urgent'. The reason people do not get on with new business contacting is that they always think they will catch up tomorrow. If you shift it into the red file for Important and Urgent, then it is today's priority).

3. Not important but can appear urgent: interruptions, some calls, mail, some reports, some meetings, many current pressing matters, many popular activities. These could be in a green file.

4. Not important, not urgent: trivia, busy work, some mail, some phone calls, many pleasant activities. These could be in the same green file, being similar in nature.

Successful companies spend about 30 per cent of their time in important and urgent, and 70 per cent in important, not urgent.

Unsuccessful companies spend more time in crisis mode and in trivia/busy work.

To repeat: unfortunately, number two, the 'important, not urgent' area, is often the one that gets the least attention. New-business activities fall in this area all too often. People mean to get on with it, but somehow they are too busy. They are always going to do it when this pressing job is over, when they get back from holidays, on Fridays when the phone stops ringing . . .

But new business is important and urgent for the simple reason that 20 to 40 per cent of our clients disappear every year from natural causes.

We do NOT have to do anything to lose this business; it just moves, merges, closes down, whatever. If you are not constantly doing new business, you are constantly closing yourself down.

Preparation time for meetings is too often done in the car or the plane. And who has time to prepare properly for a business plan, a strategic purpose for the future?—let alone revise it constantly in view of the changing nature of the world!

Yet planning is the key to the future, and the objectives within the plan are the control factor in our time management processes. If you know what your objectives are, they guide your activities, and you say 'no' to interruptions from a position of strength.

In nearly twenty years of listening to and researching company issues, I found the worldwide problem is lack of planning, or if planning is done, of implementing those plans. And worse still, even when planning is done, there is little, if any, involvement at the coalface level. One or two key people do the planning, the rest of the staff struggle along doing the best they can—reactively.

A recent client, the second largest in the world in their field, explained how the planning was done for their sales team. The product managers went away and did it together, then told the sales team what they were to do.

The sad part is of course that the product managers don't get out and sell, so how can they possibly know what it is like out there? The salespeople, therefore, had no respect for their 'plans'.

Crisis prevention, rather than putting out fires, takes planning, too. So often we hope that things will go away: things like the recession, confused and disorganised government regulations, staff resignations, out-of-control costs, gradual

'Doing the right thing seems to be more important than doing things right.'
Peter Drucker

disappearance of the traditional marketplace. Acknowledging these issues is hard, not to mention finding solutions.

Values clarification can mean hours or days meditating on one subject: what are the corporate and personal values you bring to your staff and clients/customers? How do you express these values, instil them, maintain them? Are you being true to yourself, or paying lip service to the flavour of the month?

'The computer is down. I hope it is something serious.'
Stanton Delaplane

Relationship-building is what the business and personal world is about. Given a choice, people always do business with people they like and trust. If the urgent and trivial matters of the day are preventing the development of that very important part of your life, then how can the business grow?

True recreation, doing the things you love to do, is needed to regenerate. We're talking here not of the things you think you should do, only of the things you love to do. If walking is preferable to running, dancing better than swimming, listening to music at home more enjoyable than going out to a concert, then walk, dance and listen at home.

Be good to yourself and you will feel your whole being regenerate.

In looking at the four listings of Stephen Covey's matrix, we can see how easily the activities of one, three and four prevent us from spending much time in two. But the fact is that spending a good part of our time in two is where the success of our business lies.

Plan to be ruthless about your time; work towards your objectives and say firmly, 'No, not now, but I can later', in a fair, effective and efficient way that suits your needs.

In support of your effective time management, whatever kind of business you're in, whatever the size of your company, good record-keeping is important.

You may not have the luxury of a full-time assistant, but you can be well organised all the same and have efficient methods for keeping track of essential information. The following suggestions have proved helpful.

Filing

If you deal with many different products, regions, departments or sales teams, it helps to colour-code your filing system. For example, each region would have a different colour file folder. When you see, say, a yellow file folder in your 'In' tray, you know at once that it concerns the northern region.

You will find files much more easily this way than by working through a stack of buff-coloured folders reading their individual labels. Keep file labels the same colour as the folder, so you can go straight to the relevant folders when they are hanging together in the file cabinet.

Keep a few sheets of coloured paper in your personal organiser that correspond to the colours of your project files, so that you can write your notes on the appropriate paper and find them quickly in a meeting.

Reading material

If you're going to penetrate a business niche effectively by positioning yourself as the 'expert company', you will want to stay on top of any and all information about your clients and their problems. Subscribe to all the magazines to which your clients subscribe.

Give a list of key words and topics to a junior staff person and assign that individual to the consistent task of clipping articles, highlighting them, colour-coding them to indicate in which category they should be filed and circulating them to the relevant staff.

'An intellectual is a person whose mind watches itself.'
Albert Camus (1913–1960)

This activity serves several purposes. First, it is a pipeline through which your staff can be kept fresh and vibrant, using the right jargon and conveying in every way to your clients that 'we're the right company for you'.

Second, your assistant can separate the wheat from the chaff so that you won't be wasting valuable time reading articles from which there is nothing new to learn.

Third, culling through reading material helps that person learn, which in turn makes for a more valuable assistant. Finally, it is simpler to have a folder of relevant articles to take home with you at the end of the day or the week, rather than a heavy stack of magazines.

If magazine circulation within your business takes too long, consider subscribing to your own copy of really important publications. You lose your advantage if your information-gathering lags too far behind.

GOOD ORGANISATIONAL TECHNIQUES

Reminder, Follow-up and To-Do lists can save your business. List-making is an important component of staying sane. A computer software package that allows you to keep a running list and to delete completed items is ideal.

If you don't have access to a computer, the following manual method might be a help: At the end of each day, prepare a To-Do list for the next day, highlighting the items that are a priority. At the end of the day, cross off the completed items and make up a new list for the next day.

To-Do lists can be kept in an organiser or a diary and the priorities should be clearly focused on achieving the objectives of your business and promotional plans. Everything else (except personal well-being and family matters) is probably just a distraction to those plans.

On Friday review the lists of that week to see what issues remain open. If you find that one issue keeps coming up on your list, decide whether it can be dropped altogether, or whether it must be dealt with now.

If you have been procrastinating (and who doesn't?), make that item a priority for the next working day.

KEY POINTS TO REMEMBER

- Manage your office work, staff and your time by focusing on your business plan objectives.
- Be sure to plan for personal recreation and family time. Otherwise you may well end up sick and alone. Remember, nobody ever died wishing they had spent more time in the office!
- If your business and marketing plans are realistic, congruent, relevant and flexible, don't let others change your goals and paths for superficial, unresearched reason.

'Things to do today—find the list.'
Betty Johnson

Here's what the Cornell School of Hotel Management has to say on that subject:

'Prepare yourself to take advantage of opportunities, but never take an opportunity for which you are not well prepared. When you do take up an opportunity, be involved. The biggest danger is to become a figurehead and have your assistants and admin people (in)effectively running your business.'

Don't pretend you know everything. Do not use fear tactics. If you must criticise your staff, do it positively.'

Use the problem-solving model that goes with the SWOT analysis (see Growth Skill 11) to consistently achieve constructive criticism and a well-thought-out solution).

■ ■ ■

Now to Growth Skill 10 in order to understand those around you and to thus live an easier, more exciting life.

GROWTH SKILL 10
KEEP YOUR CLIENTS (AND STAFF) FOREVER BY UNDERSTANDING THEIR PERSONALITY STYLES

For me one of the most important aspects of success is understanding the different personalities. I spent most of my life thinking that people were doing 'it' to annoy me. Then I learned that people have their own reasons for their point of view and it is over to me to listen, to see their point of view and to accommodate their feelings and needs too.

> 'People who think they know everything are very irritating to those of us who do.'
> **Unknown**

The chart on the following page will help you determine how your personal style relates to the styles of your prospects, clients, staff, friends, family and associates. Make a first pass at checking off the type you resemble the most. The people listed beside, over, or under your own square are the ones you are likely to handle best. The ones diagonally opposite are the ones with whom you are unlikely to get on in business. However, people very often marry across the diagonals because they admire qualities that they don't have themselves.

The tests on the pages will help you decide on your personality profile and that of your associates.

OVERVIEW OF THE FOUR MAIN PROFILES:
Enquirers (Chief accountant types)

Need lots of detail; like to have everything on file. Until

This section matches up with Growth Skils 2 and 6, using the same British Telecom designations for the different personality types.

they trust you they award projects only, then the entire job.

Workspace is activity-oriented. Walls may be decorated with marks of achievement. Office is organised and work-oriented. Contact between people is businesslike.

Admirers (Human resources types)

Warm, friendly, chatty, need to talk for at least twenty minutes before getting down to business.

You will get their business if you are 'one of them', and your service benefits the **people** of their organisation.

Overall atmosphere is friendly and open. Look for posters and personal items on walls and desks. Office is neat and functional. Contact between people is friendly and open. Lots of family photos.

Aspirers (Entrepreneurial types)

Brisk, to the point, want the whole picture now. Admire efficiency, speed; make decisions rapidly without proper research.

Efficiency is the theme. Walls may have an appropriate picture or achievement award, but no posters or slogans. Office is activity-oriented with a lot of work materials. Desk may be in a dominant position.

Inspirers (Visionaries, heads of big companies)

Have big ideas, need lots of variety, are easily bored, don't like to be bothered with detail.

You will get their business if you delight them with your humour, brilliance, good sense of fun.

General theme is about motivation. Walls may be covered with posters and slogans. Atmosphere is friendly and open. Desk may look cluttered. Contact between people is open. Follow through is limited. A lot of talk, little action.

'After a year in therapy my psychiatrist said to me, "Maybe life isn't for everyone."'
Larry Brown

YOUR PERSONALITY PROFILE—STRENGTHS

Unless you have already done the following exercise in connection with Growth Skill 2, please mark off **one word on each line across** that you feel most aptly describes you at work or ask a workmate to fill it in. Don't think too long, just do it as quickly and as honestly as you can.

Higher energy people		Lower energy people	
1. Animated	Persuasive	Planner	Adaptable
2. Refreshing	Sure	Orderly	Peaceful
3. Cheerful	Daring	Idealistic	Submissive
4. Demonstrative	Adventurous	Perfectionist	Considerate
5. Bouncy	Independent	Self-sacrificing	Respectful
6. Playful	Decisive	Controlled	Satisfied
7. Spontaneous	Tenacious	Sensitive	Patient
8. Delightful	Chieftain	Faithful	Shy
9. Sociable	Bold	Musical	Obliging
10. Outspoken	Competitive	Loyal	Friendly
11. Funny	Self-reliant	Analytical	Diplomatic
12. Talkative	Positive	Persistent	Consistent
13. Convincing	Mover	Reserved	Inoffensive
14. Spirited	Leader	Scheduled	Dry humour
15. Promoter	Productive	Cultured	Mediator
16. Inspiring	Strong-willed	Mapmaker	Tolerant
17. Easy mixer	Resourceful	Balanced	Listener
18. Cute	Optimistic	Detailed	Contented
19. Popular	Forceful	Thoughtful	Permissive
20. Lively	Confident	Deep	Well-behaved

** ....

Inspirer	Aspirer	Enquirer	Admirer
Corporate Head	Entrepreneur	Accountant	Human Resources

Add up the number of words you have ticked in each column *down* and write the final count in the space above marked **.

156 • *Choose and Grow Your Own Business in 90 Days*

YOUR PERSONALITY PROFILE—WEAKNESSES

Again, answer on the basis of how you behave at work or get a workmate to fill this in. Remember to tick one only in each line across.

	Higher energy people		**Lower energy people**	
1.	Brassy	(Impatient)	Reluctant	Fussy
2.	Undisciplined	Unpopular	Plain ordinary	(Too sensitive)
3.	Naive	Headstrong	(Worrier)	Doubtful
4.	Inconsistent	(Easily angered)	Low energies	Loner
5.	Messy	(Bossy)	Sluggish	Insecure
6.	Haphazard	(Unsympathetic)	Revengeful	Pessimistic
7.	Disorganised	(Resentful)	Compromising	Negative
8.	Forgetful	Tactless	(Fearful)	Withdrawn
9.	Unpredictable	(Stubborn)	Uninvolved	Moody
10.	(Argumentative)	Lordly	Suspicious	Selfish
11.	Show-off	Restless	Introvert	(Critical)
12.	Interruptive	(Proud)	Indecisive	Hard to please
13.	Permissive	(Edgy/nervy)	Timid	Slow to respond
14.	Wants credit	Workaholic	(Mumbles)	Unaffectionate
15.	Talkative	(Domineering)	Lazy	Alienated
16.	Loud	(Intolerant)	Blank	Indifferent
17.	Scatterbrain	(Short-tempered)	Unforgiving	Sceptical
18.	Rash	Crafty	Hesitant	(Bashful)
19.	Changeable	(Manipulative)	Nonchalant	Unenthusiastic
20.	Resistant	(Frank)	Depressed	Repetitious

** .... 1 .... 13 .... 3 3

Inspirer	Aspirer	Enquirer	Admirer
Visionary/	Entrepreneur	Accountant	Human Resource

Add up the number of words you have ticked in each column down and write the final count in the space above**.

Turnover to combine your strengths and weaknesses.

Strengths.	3	6	10	1
Weaknesses	1	13	3	3
Total				
Inspirer 4	Aspirer 19	Enquirer 13	Admirer 4
Visionary/	Entrepreneur	Accountant	Human
Head of Large			Resources
Corpn			

Now that you have combined the scores for the strengths and weaknesses of your personality style, your most dominant style is the column with the top mark. Your back-up style is your next highest score.

Although a person may be fairly evenly spread among three, or even all four styles, usually you will be very strongly one or two.

Your second highest score, your back-up style, tends to be the one you revert to in your spare time when the serious work of the week is over.

You can use the same analysis to define your clients, customers and prospects, but it might be easier to begin with people you know well.

See if this profile analysis helps you to understand why your differing strengths attract them and your weaknesses annoy them.

And now for more information on these various personality styles and how they behave as client, customer or prospect.

Aspirers (entrepreneurs) as clients

Code names: **The extrovert, the talker, the optimist.**

They want the whole picture now, together with organisation, practical solutions and quick action.

They delegate readily when others have proved absolutely trustworthy, but insist on goal and time setting. They thrive on opposition, have little need for friends, are usually right (!) and excel in emergencies.

Strengths: Dynamic, active, good at correcting wrongs, not easily discouraged, exude confidence, can run anything, have a strong need for change, born to lead.

Weaknesses: Not very tolerant of mistakes/fools, do not analyse detail, make rash decisions, are bored by trivia, may be rude and tactless, are demanding, believe the end justifies the means.

Enquirers (accountants) as clients
Code names: **The introvert, the pessimist, the thinker.**

They are schedule-oriented, perfectionists and detail-conscious. Orderly and organised, they hunt for economical solutions and they like graphs, charts, figures and lists.

Strengths: Deep, thoughtful, analytical, serious, purposeful, talented, creative, beauty-loving, self-sacrificing, idealistic, sensitive.

Weaknesses: Enquiries are prone to choose difficult work, not people-oriented, hesitant about starting projects, hard to please with standards that are often too high, critical of others, need approval badly, hold back affection, dislike opposition, suspicious and unforgiving, martyr-prone, tend to hypochondria.

'A team effort is a lot of people doing what I say.'
**Michael Winner,
British film director**

Admirers (human resources types) as clients
Code names: **The introvert, the watcher, the pessimist.**

They are competent and steady, peaceful and agreeable, with good administrative abilities. They avoid conflict, solve problems and come into their own under pressure. They are good listeners, have many friends and contacts, are compassionate and concerned, quick to look for the easiest way.

Strengths: Low-key in personality, easygoing, relaxed, cool, calm and collected, persistent, well-balanced, patient, quiet, witty, able to hide emotions. An all-purpose type, they make good clients because they can take the good with the bad and do not get upset easily. Since they are not in too much of a hurry, you have time to do a good job for them.

Weaknesses: Unenthusiastic, indecisive, tend to avoid responsibility, selfish, self-righteous, too compromising yet resentful about being pushed, sometimes lazy, prefer to watch rather than participate, tend to dampen enthusiasm, lack discipline, can be sarcastic and teasing.

Inspirers (visionaries, heads of large organisations) as clients

Code names: **The extrovert, the talker, the optimist.**

'The volume of
paper expands to fill
the available
briefcases.'
Jerry Brown

They apologise readily, do not hold a grudge, thrive on compliments. They love spontaneous activities and lots of people, are open to big ideas, anxious to make you feel at home, quick to think up new activities and projects, creative and colourful, bursting with energy and enthusiasm.

Strengths: They have an excellent sense of humour, are the life of the party, emotional, enthusiastic, expressive, curious, now-centred but quick to change disposition, always a child, always good at heart.

Weaknesses: Forgetful of names and obligations, undisciplined, off-putting by reason of their huge energy and enthusiasm; do not follow through, talk and laugh loudly, are easily distracted, quick to interrupt, wasteful of time, apt to confuse priorities, lose confidence easily, are naive, keep the office in a frenzy.

Ways we can modify our own behaviour

Now that we know our strengths and weaknesses, how do we make our dealings with other people more effective?

Aspirers (entrepreneurs) maintain a high-assertive, low-responsive behaviour, want to stick to their business and work independently.

Aspirers tend to be blunt, overbearing, competitive and impatient, wanting to control situations and people. If you are an aspirer, appropriate behaviour modifications would be to:

—develop empathy;

—learn to relax and pace yourself;

—be willing to listen and understand the feelings of others;

—develop patience.

Enquirers (accountants) maintain a low-assertive, low-responsive behaviour, want to stick to the facts and get down to business without any chit-chat. They follow procedures to the letter, are very conservative and analytical, resistant to change. If you are an Enquirer, appropriate behaviour modifications would be to:

—develop an understanding of the importance of feelings;

—learn to make decisions based on intuition and facts;

—be willing to bend the rules to accommodate others;

—take the initiative.

Admirers (human resources) maintain low-assertive, low-responsive behaviour. They beat around the bush in an effort to be kind and tolerant of others and take deliberate actions based on feelings and relationships. They can be lazy, sarcastic and teasing. If you are an Admirer, appropriate behaviour modifications would be to:

'The scientific theory I like best is that the rings of Saturn are composed entirely of lost airline baggage.'
Mark Russell

—develop a sense of urgency;

—learn self-assertion and strength of convictions;

—be willing to take the initiative;

—think before letting fly with sarcasm.

Inspirers (visionaries, heads of large organisations) maintain a high-assertive, high-responsive behaviour. They can be over-enthusiastic, over-optimistic and too hyped up. Their quick action is generally based on feelings and relationships. If you are an Inspirer, appropriate behaviour modifications would be to:

—develop emotional control;

—learn to use work time more wisely;

—be willing to analyse data and pay attention to facts;

—be objective.

STRATEGIES FOR DEALING WITH THE FOUR MAIN PERSONALITY STYLES

Aspirers (entrepreneurs)

1. **Initiating contact with Aspirers:** Aspirers seldom read introductory letters. Make your initial contact by phone. Your call should be businesslike and to the point. Introduce yourself, explain why you are calling and ask for an appointment. Confirm the meeting by letter and enclose any pre-meeting information the Aspirers request.

2. **Relating to Aspirers:** Aspirers value punctuality and efficient use of time. Be on time. Use factual evidence to establish your company's competence, get down to business in a formal manner. When Aspirers speak, focus your attention on their ideas and goals. Listen carefully and use only facts when answering any questions. Do not waste time, leave immediately business is done.

'When down in the mouth, remember Jonah. He came out alright.'
Thomas Edison
(1847–1931)

3. **Asking questions to discover Aspirers' needs:** Ask questions that are fact/results-oriented. Keep your questions open-ended and listen to the response; you won't be told twice. Support their conclusions and confirm their needs by feeding back your understanding, factually and clearly. Don't mumble, stutter, and 'hope for the best'!

4. **Showing why Aspirers should use your company:** Be specific, but don't overwhelm them with details. Offer alternative solutions and let Aspirers make their own decision from the options. One solution is not enough, they need an either/or situation.

   But don't do as I did once: I took in eight possible solutions to a woman whom I now understand to be an Aspirer. At the time she was really quite angry to have to waste her time working through so many choices. No more than three, ever, was her cry! (An Inspirer, however, might have liked the fun of debating all eight alternatives!)

5. **Supporting Aspirers' use of your company:** Let Aspirers make their decision by asking directly for their business. Be prepared to reply with facts to any concerns they have and to be clear about alternative ways of meeting their company's needs. Be willing to negotiate regarding their ideas and objectives.

'Happiness is good health and a bad memory.'
Ingrid Bergman
(1917–1982)

Enquirers (accountants)

1. **Initiating contact with Enquirers:** Start with a personal letter which gives specific information about your company. Be sure to include information about your company's background and expertise, stability and cost-effectiveness. Follow the letter with a phone call

requesting a meeting. A businesslike manner, stating how much time you will need and what you will bring with you, works well with these people.

2. **Relating to Enquirers:** Be on time. State your purpose for the visit and stick to your agenda. Enquirers will want evidence of your company's problem-solving abilities. Present your evidence in a careful and deliberate manner.

3. **Asking questions to discover Enquirers' needs:** Ask specific 'how' and 'what' questions and make copious notes on the answers. Take an unhurried approach. Encourage them to relate their feelings as to 'what' it is they are trying to achieve and 'how' it is important to the company. Summarise those factors indicated as important and be prepared for additional discussions on these matters.

4. **Showing why Enquirers should use your company:** Prepare a well-organised, detailed, written plan which offers logical, systematic approaches. Emotional appeals will not work with Enquirers. Use examples to show how your proposal will solve their particular problems. If they ask a question you cannot answer, offer to find out and get back to them. Do not pretend to know, they will sense it immediately.

5. **Supporting Enquirers' use of your company:** Use a low-key approach to ask for the order. Concerns should be addressed by appealing to their sense of value-for-money and objectivity. Be prepared to negotiate details and probably price. If you cannot yield on price now, offer a value-added deal such as a discount on payment within five working days, or volume discount after so many 'done deals'.

'Beware of those who seek to take care of you, lest your caretakers become your jailers.'
Jim Rohn

Admirers (human resources)

1. **Initiating contact with Admirers:** Initial contact should be made through a letter of introduction. Be sure to include information about your reputation, reliability and experience as well as the quality of your company's service. Follow the letter with a phone call. Take time to be friendly and establish a trusting relationship before asking for a meeting.

2. **Relating to Admirers:** Start the meeting on time with friendly chit-chat intended to establish your relationship. Admirers will be most interested in information about you and want you to be genuinely interested in information about them. Initiate the business discussion by describing how you will work to solve their problems.

> 'A committee is a cul-de-sac down which ideas are lured and then quietly strangled.'
> **Sir Barnett Cocks (c. 1907)**

3. **Asking questions to discover Admirers' needs:** Ask open-ended questions which will draw out their personal goals and needs. Clarify their feelings in your own mind by asking 'what' and 'when' questions. Admirers will expect you to listen actively by giving plenty of verbal and non-verbal feedback. When summarising, reflect your understanding of their concerns and feelings.

4. **Showing why Admirers should use your company:** Provide a clear, written solution to their needs, indicating how you will work together. They must be assured that your solution will work, now and in the future.

   Personally guarantee your proposal. Admirers will also want to know what other people think of your work, so give them the names of people they can contact, together with phone numbers, titles, company names.

5. **Supporting Admirers' use of your company:** Don't back Admirers into a corner or try to force them to make a decision. Ask for the business in an indirect manner.

'Agree, for the law
is costly.'
William Camden,
1551–1623

Listen to their concerns in a patient, peaceful way and give calm, thorough answers. The Admirer will try to avoid making a commitment, so be sure to stress your personal involvement in follow-up activities.

Inspirers (visionaries)

1. **Initiating contact with Inspirers:** Start with a phone call. To Inspirers, letters are impersonal and usually go unread. The tone of your phone call should be open and friendly. Stress your experience, personal service and (quickly) the benefits of using your company.

2. **Relating to Inspirers:** Be on time but be prepared to wait for the Inspirer; they have no use for clockwatchers. They have plenty of time for small talk and will want to build a personal relationship by swapping stories about mutual acquaintances. Get them to talk about their personal interests and relate your own feelings.

3. **Asking questions to discover Inspirers' needs:** Questions to Inspirers should be direct and probing, using 'who', 'what', 'how'. Show an active interest in their responses by providing a lot of verbal and non-verbal feedback. Your questions should help you gain specific information about their goals. As you summarise, relate your own feelings while bringing goals and needs into sharp focus.

4. **Showing why Inspirers should use your company:** Be specific and factual, but do not overwhelm them with a lot of detail. Try to keep the discussion on track without pushing too hard. Work closely to develop ideas and strategies. Inspirers are easily bored so do not stay on one subject too long.

   They have no problem with accommodating five or

ten ideas at one time and are wonderful candidates for an exciting and vibrant meeting.

5. **Supporting Inspirers' use of your company:** Always assume that you have the contract. Concerns should be dealt with by sharing stories of other people's successes through using your company.

Give exciting, vivid case studies, quick and to the point. Make your incentive a bright, new way of looking at dull and boring contracts. For instance, when a certain amount is spent with your company, offer extra product free, as opposed to, say, a volume discount.

Or give a volume discount based on an estimate of a year's buying needs. If they reach that volume, fine; if not, they owe you. However, if they go beyond that volume, you owe them money.

I have used this technique very successfully in the hotel industry. It worked so well with a good-sized supplier of room nights to the Inter-Continental Hotel, where I was sales manager, that we owed them enough money to guarantee their volume per night room rate stayed the same for the whole of the following year.

They preferred this type of refund to actual cash in hand. It turned a very average relationship into a very successful one for both parties.

> 'Even if you're on the right track, you'll get run over if you just sit there.'
> **Will Rogers**
> **(1879–1935)**

HOW THE FOUR TYPES BEHAVE UNDER STRESS

People often get stressed out by life, so you should be aware that each of us, in addition to our dominant personality style, has a back-up profile which shows itself under great stress or tension. Back-up profiles are characterised by immature reactions and behaviour.

When they are in evidence, all you can do is focus on leading that angry, upset client, prospect, friend or family member through the tension and back into the dominant personality style you are used to. **Do not take it personally. You are sorry that it happened, but it is not your fault.**

Aspirers (entrepreneurs) will behave like 'Der Fuhrer'. Aspirers like to be in control, but never more so than when stressed out. They snap out orders and decisions with no room for discussion. Facts and logic will support their rage.

The best way to deal with Der Fuhrer is to listen to the complaints with empathy and intelligent responses. Once they see that their feelings carry weight with you, you will be able to get them back to their normal Aspirer behaviour. You have shown them that they are in charge and that their decisions and feelings are important.

Enquirers (accountants) will become 'Artful Dodgers'. Their basic tendency to avoid making decisions now spreads over into all areas: they just won't deal with anything. They become curt and surly, refusing to answer questions and cutting short your responses.

'It is easier to get forgiveness than permission.' **Murphy's Law, Book 2 (P.S. O'Halloran's Law says Murphy's Laws are optimistic)**

Give them permission to speak out and say what is wrong. Simply listen. Allow them an opportunity to let off steam—and be prepared for a torrent! Agree with their feelings and offer alternatives based on some new information.

Admirers (human resources) become doormats. They deal with conflict by lying down. They will sign anything, do anything if you will just go away and leave them alone. You can expect a call later, however, cancelling the contract.

When the Admirer stops discussing things with you and says, 'Fine, do it any way you want', take time out to find out what is wrong. Suggest they dump on you and be prepared for a blazing personal attack. Anything and everything is open to attack.

Inspirers (visionaries) become spoilt brats who are displeased with everything and anything around them. They can be rude, uncooperative, blunt and angry with you, your work, your tie or dress even. Let them wear themselves out, and show that you relate to their feelings.

Nod empathetically. When the storm is over, get on with working together in a way that meets their needs. They will forgive you over a great lunch, and your note of apology goes a long way.

'I've always been interested in people, but I have never liked them.'
W. Somerset Maugham (1874–1965)

MAKE THE FOUR MAIN PERSONALITY PROFILES WORK FOR YOU

By now it is evident that there are two types of people in this world that we are discussing:

1. High energy people, who move quickly, run around a lot and speak quickly as well as making quick decisions. These are the extroverts.
2. Lower energy people, who move more slowly, talk more slowly and make decisions over a longer period of time. These are the introverts.

You can say, too, that the world is divided in two: those who are usually in their offices and usually answer their phones (the lower energy, introverted people) and those who are seldom in their offices, and seldom answer their phones (the high energy, more extroverted people).

Yet the high energy person who makes the quick decisions is the very person that the salespeople need to get to meet. So how do we achieve it?

I find they are often in their offices early in the morning, at lunch time and after work. If you can get through to them, you can sell to them, so work hard at getting their mobile phone numbers and their direct phone lines. Really spend time tracking these people down, as they are the quick deal-makers.

Stay away from accountant types and human resource types.

'Nice guys finish last, but we get to sleep in.'
Evan Davis

Although you can reach them by phone, their decision-making processes will mean you spend a long time giving them the extraordinary amount of detail or nurturing that they require, while the energetic people are buying quickly from someone else.

A client told me that she had spent months supplying an accountant type with more detail, more detail, more detail (without yet getting the business), when she could have sold at least one hundred pieces of business to her high energy prospects over the same time. She had neglected them for this seductive and elusive chase to finally give the accountant all that he needed. One day maybe!

Be aware that I am simply describing normal behaviours that differentiate the introverts and the extroverts of our world. There is no blame attached to any personality type, it is just the way we are!

And if you want to be successful in selling, you will use your energy to meet and match with people who do make quick decisions, and give you a comfortable living by so doing. Leave the slow decision-makers to your competitors, hoping they have not read this book!

Underneath the headings of the four personality styles, list as many of your clients and prospects as you can fit in

Remind yourself that these are the people you deal with on a daily basis, and choose how you want to live your selling life.

Stay with the high energy people (Aspirers and Inspirers) for quick decisions and a good life.

Aspirers (entrepreneurs)
(This personality style is the best to hire for sales as they are self-starters **and** follow through.)

Enquirers (accountants)
(Do not hire in sales as they are so information-oriented they never get enough detail and therefore cannot ask for the sale. They are, however, at their best in the accounting/admin role.)

Admirers (human resources)
(Again, do not hire in sales because they are so busy nurturing and identifying needs and discussing how they might proceed that they do not ask for the order. But they are wonderful in the HR/training/nurturing role).

Inspirers (visionaries, heads of large organisations)

(Once more, don't hire these people in sales because they are great talkers, but small doers. Their mission is to have a great time and delegate. If there is no one to delegate to, it just does not get done. Highly charismatic people, they are great in a large, successful organisation, leading it to further victories.)

NLP—NEUROLINGUISTIC PROGRAMMING

More good news: Across the world people say to me that their real problem is communication skills—or lack of them. Here is the solution.

In a recent meeting where a group of around thirty people were similarly bemoaning their inability to communicate with each other, one person said, 'What is there that you can give us that will change this problem?' and I said, 'Neurolinguistics.'

When I first learned about NLP, as it is called in its short form, I thought I had died and gone to heaven. Now as an NLP practitioner, I have the best time of my life, understanding what is going on around me, and being proactive instead of reactive. Let me give you an example:

An acquaintance called me and said that either she or her daughter had to leave home! Since her daughter is only seven, it seemed that the mother had to go, but not willingly, as she had a son with whom she had a very close, cuddly relationship—and she enjoyed her husband!

'What's the problem?' I asked, and she explained that the daughter would endlessly pull at her clothing, saying,

'Mummy, Mummy, do you love me?' And Mummy would bend down and give her a kiss, as she did for her son.

Not satisfied, the daughter would repeat the process, and her mother could no longer take the tugging and the pleading. One of them had to go.

My recommendation was that she shift from the kiss to a verbal response, such as, 'Yes, dear, I do.'

The next day I got a phone call. The daughter had come into the kitchen, asked the usual question, tugging at her mother and, on hearing the response of 'Yes, dear, I do,' said, 'Thank you, Mummy,' and ran outside to play. It was that easy.

This is NLP at work. Very simply it seems that about 40 per cent of the world gives out and takes in information visually: they see life in pictures. Love to them is shown by a caring look and by little gifts.

About 20 per cent live an auditory life; words mean everything to them, as in the case of the little seven-year-old girl who longed to hear the words, 'Yes, dear, I do.'

About 40 per cent of the world operates emotionally; they need to feel everything around them, and love means being hugged and kissed, just as the brother of the little girl thrived on his mother's hugs and kisses, all of which meant nothing to his sister.

As a friend said recently, getting on with people that you are naturally attracted to is easy. Getting on with 'irregulars', people who are wrong for you, is the challenge.

We all have these 'irregulars' in our life: people we have to work with or socialise with for business or family reasons.

Now we know how to do it: we simply use their language instead of our own. Read on to learn how you can use NLP to live a proactive life and one that is rich in successful relationships.

'Good people are good because they come to wisdom through failure.'
William Saroyan

NLP: the three languages of seeing, hearing and feeling.
The number one secret weapon for transferring information effectively is to adapt your personal communications style to that of your audience.

Neurolinguistic programming (NLP) was discovered by the famed psychoanalyst, Carl Jung. He found, through listening to his patients tell their life stories, that we humans have three different styles of hearing, each with its own matching spoken and written language.

These styles are **visual**, where we express ourselves largely in pictures; **auditory**, where we use hard-nosed facts; and **feelings**, where we speak of how we feel.

These styles enable us to communicate easily with those like us and can hinder us from communicating well with others who are not like us. As a result you may have said, felt and heard the following comments often, where your personal communication style has not matched that of the recipients:

- 'He just doesn't speak our language.'
- 'No matter how often I tell them, they just don't listen.'
- 'It's like talking to a blank wall.'
- 'They just don't get it.'
- 'None so blind as those who will not see.'
- 'It seems as though they are totally deaf.'
- 'There's nothing except blank indifference.'
- 'They're just not in touch with the issues.'

'Never go to bed mad. Stay up and fight.'
Phyllis Diller

As we said, these personal styles operate on a 40/20/40 rule:

- Forty per cent of people hear by seeing pictures as you talk to them, and use highly visual language when speaking and writing, such as:

  'I can see the whole picture now.'

  'I saw Jim last week.'

'See you soon.'

'I want to show you this . . . ,'

'Look here.'

'See what I mean?'

- Twenty per cent of people respond best to auditory words and use sound-oriented words in their speech and when they write, such as:

    'I hear you loud and clear.'

    'I spoke with Jim last week.'

    'Talk to you soon.'

    'Come and talk to me.'

    'That rings a bell.'

    'Let's talk this through.'

- Forty per cent of people respond to feeling words, and use sensitive words in their speaking and writing, such as:

    'I feel very deeply on this issue.'

    'I touched base with Jim last week.'

    'Let's get together soon.'

    'This is a sensitive issue.'

    'How do you feel about this?'

    'Stay in touch, if it's not too much trouble.'

'We must believe in luck, for how else can we explain the success of those we don't like?'
Jean Cocteau
(1889–1963)

A real life example. Friend Jo had written a letter of complaint to a department store and received a quick phone response. The company representative said, 'I can feel your anger.'

Jo was deeply insulted. She is among that 20 per cent that responds to auditory language, not that 40 per cent that responds through their feelings.

I asked Jo how she would have felt if the caller had said, 'I hear your anger,' and Jo agreed that would be fine. How about, 'I can see that you are angry'? That would have been okay as well.

Most people have a back-up language, and Jo's primary

style is auditory with a back-up style of visual. Yet, even understanding what was going on, Jo swore she would never shop at that store again. Yes, it can be that easy to lose a sale or further upset a customer or client.

It's also a good idea to use neutral language when seeking an appointment. Ask only if you can meet, not 'have an appointment to see . . .'; not 'I have a feeling we should get together'; not 'I think we should talk.'

Use language that does not trigger negative responses and your ratio of appointments to phone calls could well improve. Or you could use all three languages when asking for an appointment by saying, 'How do you feel about my coming to see you and talking through your needs?'

Another example: Imagine for a moment that three people went to visit Janet, their office manager, who has broken her leg skiing. A visual person would report back that they had great fun drawing graffiti on the cast. A hearing person, that they knocked on the cast and it sounded hollow—Janet is disappearing inside. A feeling person, that Janet is going nuts with the itchy bits inside. Same person, same cast, three different opinions, behaviours and reactions.

The second clue to the communications style of people with whom you're speaking is in their eye movement. People who are asked to remember a past occasion look up towards their eyebrows if they hear by seeing, as if seeing the picture of the previous event in their mind's eye.

If they respond by hearing, they look sideways toward their ears to hear the words of that time. If they hear by feeling, they look down toward their hearts to recapture the emotions of that time.

For instance, a prominent Australian Prime Minister was thought to be shifty because his eyes went sideways to his

'Destiny is not a matter of chance; it is a matter of choice. It is not a thing to be waited for; it is a thing to be achieved.'
William Jennings Bryan

ears when he was recalling what was said or done in the past. He was simply looking for the sound, not avoiding or lying about the issue.

Several people involved in executive recruitment remarked to me recently that they had always judged applicants to be shifty when they looked sideways before answering interview questions.

Now they realise it is a recall mode. Eyes moving up into the eyebrows or down toward the heart for visual and feeling recall do not create the same shifty impression; they are simply seen as normal eye movements, if noticed at all.

Of course, if you are making a presentation to a room full of people, you can't watch them all for these clues and still remember what you're trying to say! Therefore, make sure your presentation addresses each communication style. Add more descriptive words and sounds into your verbal presentations, include relevant background music and sounds; try to capture the eyes, ears, hearts (and minds) of 100 per cent of your listeners.

'I don't care what is written about me, so long as it isn't true.'
Dorothy Parker

Otherwise, you can lose between 60 and 80 per cent of them by using your own preferred speaking style. Adjust to your audience as you would try to do in a foreign country. If you want to eat, sleep, fill up the car, buy medical supplies or ask directions, it really helps if you know the words in their language.

In the same way, our presentations come alive for all those people sitting there, judging our best work. By using all of the three languages of your audience, you enrol the whole room, rather than a small piece.

It has been said that usually about 25 per cent of the room is listening, the other 75 per cent are somewhere between apathy and deep dislike. No longer—now you can have

100 per cent of people listening, empathising and buying into your presentations.

For example, you are presenting an advertising campaign for a new range of leisure wear linked to an outdoor lifestyle. Perhaps you will be showing boards with pictures on them, to represent your T.V. campaign. Your storyboards would show people wearing Janna's leisure clothes against the backdrop of Sydney's Harbour Bridge, Opera House and waterways, enhanced by trains, ships, small craft and racing yachts. Or you could use an anamatic, being lively drawings on video. Either way, a voice tells the story. And of course the clothes are on show. It is very visual at this stage.

If you were a person with a visual communication style, you would probably automatically use this kind of visual language to describe the T.V. commercial:

'The glitter of the speeding trains on the bridge, the cool whiteness of the Opera House under the bright sun, the colourful yachts under full spinnaker and the waves foaming around the bow . . . Janna's leisure wear is seen at its best advantage.'

If hearing language came naturally to you, you would perhaps talk of 'the clickety-clack of the trains, the sound of the music in the Opera House, the hiss of the waves as the yachts cut through the water, racing to the starting line, and the crack and slap of the sails as they changed direction . . . Janna's leisure wear captures the applause of the weekend set.'

And if you were someone who naturally used feeling language, you might talk about 'being on the most beautiful harbour in the world, close to the great performers at the Opera House; the delight of the wind in our hair and the sun on our faces as we hold the tiller, fighting for the starting position . . . Janna's leisure wear has that certain feeling.'

Now here is an example of how you can use all three languages at once to enrol the whole audience in your pitch:

'As the silver train clatters across the bridge, a vista unfolds. The Opera House gleams white in the bright Sydney sun, the famous voices within echoing in our minds. Yachts under brightly coloured spinnakers speed to the line. The boom of the starting gun tells us the race is on. We can taste the salt on our lips, feel the wind in our hair, the sun on our faces. A great lifestyle invites us in as we see, hear and feel the pleasure of Janna's new collection.'

Backed by the right music, interspersed with the clickety-clack of trains, the voices of famous opera singers, the hiss of the waves, the starting-gun shot, your presentation will now involve everyone in the room, and particularly those who respond with their ears.

These people are the most difficult of all to sway, these 20 per cent! They truly have to hear it to believe it. Then of course the others have to see it to believe and have to feel that the campaign is right for the product.

'Are you going to come quietly or do I have to wear ear plugs?'
From the Goon Show

How does this knowledge of neurolinguistics apply in getting new business?

During a recent pitch, I knew that two out of the three people in the room were entirely with me. The third was sitting back in his chair, arms folded, frowning in disbelief. I had been talking about the importance of NLP in helping to win new business, but John was not convinced.

'What is my style?' he asked. Because it was a small group, I had managed to pick up his eye movements, so I replied that he was possibly auditory.

'How will you convince me?' he demanded. I replied, 'By giving you the names and numbers of people whom you can phone, so that you can hear through your ears that this technique is successful.'

A moment of silence, then he laughed, and I now had three people in the room who were in agreement with me.

It's not so difficult to use all three language styles at once if you are already a good communicator. The examples that follow will help you decide how many of the three languages you are currently using. You can be successful with an extraordinary number of new-business pitches by remembering the 40/20/40 Rule and adapting your personal style to that of others.

How does this knowledge of neurolinguistics apply in enriching your personal life?

Let's consider 'Love Strategies' for analysing what makes you and others feel truly loved.

'Some things have to be believed to be seen.'
Ralph Hodgson
on ESP

The study of neurolinguistics shows us that when we fall in love we use all three languages at the same time. We see love in our beloved's eye, and they in ours, we bring gifts, we whisper sweet nothings and oh, the towering feeling of the hugs, the lovemaking, the nibbling and stroking.

Then time goes by and it's no longer the same; it seems that love has died. Why? Because after the first flush of excitement, each of us reverts to our preferred and back-up style. If our partner has the same styles, all is well because we settle well into friendship and mutual respect. Otherwise we break up, move on, looking again for that special person who will understand us, make us feel loved again. Or else we stay, wishing things were different but without the skills to know what the problem is.

For instance, a highly feeling man will long for hugs, for touch; his highly visual partner will long for flowers, for little gifts. An auditory woman will say, 'He no longer loves me'—the proof being that he doesn't tell her so anymore.

Recently I spoke to a young woman, now divorced. I asked her what went wrong. She explained that as her husband came home from work, he made a beeline for her. She, with three children underfoot wanting their dinner, dreaded his arrival.

Her comment was, 'He couldn't even **see** that I was trying to get dinner and do you know, he never even **brought me a flower from my own garden**.' A highly feeling man with a highly visual woman—and had either of them known what was going on, they might have compromised. He with a flower before dinner, she with affection after dinner.

Here we have a couple of lost people wondering why it was-n't working after being so in love only a few years ago. I asked her husband what went wrong and he said, '**She never said please, she just told me to do things**.' It hurt his feelings to be 'told'—and since he didn't bring her flowers, they divorced.

Let me tell you about the love strategy of a young woman volunteer at a seminar in Sydney. Up on the stage in front of 1200 people, Tony Robbins asked her what had to happen for her to feel absolutely loved.

Did she have to see it in the eyes of her beloved, in the gifts that he brought? No. Did she have to hear it in the words that he said? No. Did she have to feel it in a certain way? YES!

What was that certain way? She explained that 'he' would have to come to her, place his fingertips over her cupped, upward-facing fingers then oh! so gently put his arms around her and hold her to him. Then she would feel absolutely loved.

Assuming that she was no longer with that man who made her feel so loved, how much chance would she have of ever feeling loved by another man—unless that man happened to be in the audience that night!

'The doctor can bury his mistakes, but an architect can only advise his clients to plant vines.'
Frank Lloyd Wright

So what is your love strategy? Think back to a time when you felt absolutely loved or loving. Did you have to see it, to hear it, or to feel it?

Many of us would say all three, yet there is usually one that you could not bear to be without. Would you give up the shining, loving look in their eyes for words and a hug? Perhaps, perhaps not.

Would you give up the words, 'I love you,' for the gifts, the shining eyes, the hugs? Perhaps, perhaps not.

Would you give up the hugs for words, for gifts, for loving eyes? Perhaps, perhaps not.

When you have identified your preferred way of being loved, ask yourself if you know your partner's, and if not, what would change if you did. I know a woman whose husband brings her flowers every Friday night, and every Friday night there is a special dinner cooked, just for the two of them.

And remember, too, that every person you meet in business or in friendship has a preferred way of feeling loved. They too have the emotional needs that you and I have. They may like little gifts, or they may feel 'bought.'

> 'A little inaccuracy sometimes saves tons of explanation.'
> **H.H. Munro (Saki)**
> **(1870–1916)**

They may like to hear words of admiration, or they may feel manipulated.

They may like a warm touch, or they may feel affronted.

It may sound like a minefield, but people send out signals all the time. Now that you are receptive to these signals, the answers will come through loud and clear; you will see and feel and hear what is going on.

Remember when we were children and we sniffed the breeze on arriving home? We knew instantly what mood the adults were in, how we should adapt in order to survive! You can do it now that you are an adult—the skills are still there, just waiting to be used again.

The Managing Director of Nando's Chickenland (now a successful worldwide franchise operation) tells the story of how he nearly lost the business.

At that typical stage where he needed extra funding for the expansion of his home-grown success story, bank after bank after bank refused him those extra dollars, the officials never even looking up from their desks at his excellent visual presentation.

As the MD said later, he presented in his own visual style, instead of the style the bankers require, and that is to deliver (auditory style) hard-nosed facts from well-researched and profit-directed facts and documents.

Fortunately, another more visual source understood the company's need (no, not a banker) and the rest is history.

One of the larger companies in in-house catering tells of a similar experience. They spent a lot of money on slides, showing the banking group concerned how well they would run the executive and staff dining rooms.

As the head of the catering company said, 'The bankers sat there with their heads down. The only way I could get them to look up was to stop speaking, but the moment I started again, they dropped their heads.'

Awarded the business, they sent in an evaluation form, and one banker scrawled across it, 'You certainly did NOT get the business from your presentation.' In my course on NLP they realised, as had Nando's MD, that they had used their own very visual language, for auditory bankers.

NLP helps you understand when you have made a mistake, and how you can avoid making it again.

Interested in learning more? Turn over the page to Growth Skill 10A.

> 'What we call real estate—the solid ground to build a house on—is the broad foundation on which nearly all the guilt of the world rests.'
> **Nathaniel Hawthorn (1804–1864)**

GROWTH SKILL 10A: NLP TRAINING PROGRAM

Interested in learning more?

This is the program I use when consulting for companies on NLP. You need to have at least two people to use this material well. This comes with special thanks to all my NLP teachers.

Objectives

By doing these exercises you will likely learn:

- A new model of human behaviour and communication.
- How people represent, decode, and process information internally.
- To communicate so your message is easily understood.
- Predictable ways of establishing and maintaining rapport with any individual.
- Concepts and applications of non-verbal communication.
- Individual personality preferences and distinctions.
- How to avoid miscommunications.

Agenda:

Introduction

Establishing Rapport

1. Matching representational systems
2. Eye accessing
3. What communicates your message?
4. Matching voice qualities
5. Non-verbal communication
6. Personality distinctions

Influencing Others

7. Pacing and leading

8. Outcome/problem frame

9. Eliciting and utilising criteria

10. Anchoring techniques

Introduction

List the challenges you face, at home and at work, where your ability to influence others is important to your success.

The learning process

1. When we are born we are unconsciously incompetent. We do not know how to do anything, and do not care! We simply make a fuss until someone comes along and fixes it.

2. As we get older we realise that we are struggling to do the simplest things, like feed ourselves, crawl, walk, run, speak. We are conscious of our incompetence and do care—hence the tears, tantrums, terrible twos.

3. Later we are consciously competent: we can read slowly, walk and talk carefully, feed ourselves somewhat, do up our buttons and tie our shoelaces—but we have to think about it as we do it.We can write, but only with a tightly gripped pencil and our tongue poking out.

4. Then as more time goes by, we become unconsciously competent: we can read, eat, walk, run, drive, and do many other things without thinking. We have reached a

new maturity. But every new skill we take on board has to start first with the semi-conscious or conscious awareness that we are incompetent at something, that we want to change to a better way of life.

We have to want to change or else we don't focus, learn, take on board the new ways. Hence we become very good at doing things that we have a passion or real liking for, and remain consciously incompetent at the things we dislike.

List some of the things you love to do and do well.

And some things you dislike doing and do badly.

Our goal is to learn more techniques for increasing sales, to become unconsciously competent at selling. NLP is the key.

Understanding Representational Systems

Each of us experiences a constant stream of information being communicated to us by way of sensory communication channels. We communicate with one another most frequently by using the three primary senses: visual or sight, auditory or sound, and kinesthetic or feelings or touch.

We call these sensory channels **representational systems** because they represent how a person is receiving external information and making sense of it internally.

People who communicate via **visual** representational systems **see** pictures and have images of their experiences.

People who communicate via **auditory** representational systems **hear** sounds and talk about their experiences.

People who communicate via their **kinaesthetic** system experience internal or external sensations and have **feelings** about their experiences.

Equally important is the fact that not only do we see, hear, and feel experiences being communicated to us from an external source, but the psychoanalyst Carl Jung heard in his counselling sessions that we also express such experiences by using specific language patterns which indicate the representational system we are using.

The words comprising such language patterns are called 'predicates' and include verbs, adjectives and adverbs, which are the parts of speech used for showing action, describing something, and telling how, when, and where.

People who describe their experiences visually usually use predicates such as 'look', 'see', 'picture', or 'perspective'.

People who describe their experiences in an auditory way use predicates such as 'hear', 'say', 'listen', 'sound', or 'talk'.

People who describe their experiences kinaesthetically use such predicates as 'feel', 'hold', 'handle', or 'grasp'. Often, we unconsciously use the sensory-based language that someone else is using; we match each other's representational system and become easily absorbed in conversation.

However, there are times when we unconsciously 'mismatch' someone else's representational system and then wonder why no rapport was established.

The biggest block to rapport is thinking that because you see the world one way, everyone else does too. Excellent communicators rarely make that mistake. They know they have to change their language, their tonality, their gestures, until they discover an approach that is successful in achieving their outcome.'
Anthony Robbins, Unlimited Power

Herein lies the difference between people who easily establish rapport and trust with others and those who do not.

In order to successfully establish high levels of rapport with another person, it is important to be able to identify and match the specific representational system or language patterns used to communicate.

By doing this, the outcome of a given situation will be the establishment of rapport and trust with the person, thereby improving the quality of your relationship.

The benefits you derive from this ability can be utilised in every area of your personal and professional life.

Describe in your own words a time when you felt in total rapport with another person—where you were, what you were doing, why it was special:

_____

_____

Examples of words that reveal representational systems.

The following examples of sensory-specific predicates reveal the various representational systems by which we communicate.

Visual

- I **see** what you are saying.
- That **looks** good.
- This idea isn't **clear.**
- I'm **hazy** about that.
- I went **blank.**

- Let's cast some **light** on the subject.
- Get a new **perspective.**
- Looking back, it **appears** differently.
- It was an **enlightening, (insightful, colourful)** example.

Auditory

- I **hear** you.
- It **rings** a bell.
- It **sounds** good to me.
- Everything suddenly **clicked.**
- **Listen** to yourself.
- The idea has been **rattling** around in my head.
- Something **tells** me to be careful.
- I can really **tune** into what you're saying.

Kinaesthetic

- It **feels** right to me.
- Get a **handle** on it.
- Do you **grasp** the basic concept?
- Get in **touch** with yourself.
- I have a **solid** understanding of it.
- I'm **up against** a wall.
- **Change** your standpoint.
- You're so **insensitive.**
- I have a **feeling** you're right.
- I am **boxed** into a corner.

'We can't all be heroes because somebody has to sit on the curb and clap as they go by.'
Will Rogers (1879–1935)

A person reading a vacation brochure could be representing their future experience in a variety of ways. They may see the sights of the holiday, imagine the sounds and tastes of skiing, swimming, sailing, drinking, eating, and feel the sensations of all those activities, but at different levels of intensity.

Some more practice:

In the following examples of representational systems, mark off those phrases that you would feel comfortable using in everyday language.

Visual

- Lazy, **hazy** days of summer
- This is an **obscure** and difficult text
- It is all too **dim** and in the past
- I agree with your **perspective**
- We have let minor issues **cloud** our thinking
- We gained **focus** through reviewing the document
- The **picture** is clear now
- **Envision** this new equipment
- She is remarkable for her **vision**
- We all have a different **viewpoint**
- From my point of **view**
- Come **look** at this
- **Gaze** out the window
- **Illuminate** us with your wisdom
- Get a **glimpse** of this
- Let me **illustrate** that point
- We **perceive** them to be different
- We will keep **watch** on their progress
- Let them first **scan** the information
- We need to **survey** the results first
- The effect is **visible**
- We can **see** the whole **picture** at a **glance**
- The longer we **stare** at the mess, the less it will go away
- **Show** me how you did it
- That **looks pretty good** to me
- Now I have got the **picture**

- It is as **clear as mud**
- The **after-glow** of a great presentation

Auditory

- **Hear** me out
- You are not **listening** to me
- **Talk** me through the problem
- I'm in **harmony** with your needs
- It's coming through **loud** and **clear**
- **Shout** it out
- I **told** you that would happen
- Post-purchase **dissonance** is allowed for in the contract
- A **resounding yell**
- Lend an **ear**
- I bent his **ear**
- You need to **amplify** that point
- **Chatter box**
- **Whine and groan**
- All you ever do is **moan**
- **Hiss** and foam of the sea
- He **voiced** his opinion
- We must **orchestrate** the presentation
- **Sounds** like fun out there
- The **silence** is killing me
- I'm in **tune** with your ideas
- **Tone** down the extravagance

'It is only possible to live happily ever after on a day to day basis.'
Margaret Bonnano

Kinaesthetic

- **Feel** the **feeling**
- So **warm** to **touch**
- Can you **handle** the problem?
- **Grasp the nettle**

- A **tight** ship is a good ship
- **Smooth** as silk
- **Rough and tumble** of business
- **Cut and thrust** of negotiation
- A **firm** hand at the helm
- Apply **pressure** if they don't decide soon
- Their **indecision** makes the situation tense
- **Concrete** evidence
- **Hurt feelings**
- Handled **roughly**
- He is **clumsy** with figures
- She is **relaxed** about deadlines
- It's a **swell** world we live in
- **Tremble** at the sound of his voice
- **Shiver** all over at that piece of music
- **Shake** them up, get them going
- **Penetrate** the puffery
- **Absorb** the cost and fix the problem
- **Uncomfortable** with dissent
- **Stir** the masses
- **Agitated** by lack of timeliness
- **Cutting** remarks
- **Glow** with pride
- **Flush** with happiness
- **Itch** to succeed
- **Creep** up unannounced

Olfactory/ Gustatory (smell/taste)
- **Sweet** taste of success
- The **flavour** of the month
- **Savour** the moment
- **Relish** the thought

- Nice and **tangy**
- A **palatable** offer
- Leaves a **nasty aftertaste**
- The **sweet smell** of success
- **Scent** the breeze
- A **whiff** of how it could be
- **Pungent** with desire
- The contract **stinks**
- There's a **reek** of deceit
- A **nose** for a good deal
- Leave a **bad taste** in my mouth

'In the race to be better or best, do not miss the joy of being.'
Unknown

Predicate Exercise 1.

Identify which system is being used in the following sentences. Place a 'V' for Visual, 'A' for Auditory and 'K' for Kinaesthetic beside each indented phrase.

I understand you . . .
- What you are doing **feels** right to me
- I **see** what you mean
- I **hear you loud and clear**

I know . . .
- I can **grasp** your meaning
- That really **clicks**
- I'm in **tune** with what you're doing
- That's **clear** to me
- That **fits** in
- I **catch** the idea
- That **rings** a bell
- I have gained **insight**
- I **see** your point

- That **strikes** me as being correct
- That's perfectly clear

That's confusing . . .
- **Show** it to me in black and white
- I can't make rhyme nor **reason** of it
- I'm trying to **take it in**
- **Sounds** like **noise** to me

I don't understand . . .
- It's **dim**
- It **sounds** distorted
- I can't get **in touch** with your needs

It seems obscure . . .
- It doesn't **fit in**
- It's all very **hazy** to me
- That point is as **clear as mud**
- It **sounds** garbled

Help me to understand . . .
- It has **slipped away** from me
- It's all **Greek** to me
- I'm **straining** to get your meaning
- It **sounds** like **gibberish**
- I don't **see** your meaning

Predicate Exercise II

Mark each phrase as being an example of V, A, K, or O/G.
- I **feel** like I'm dealing with too many people
- We **perceive** promotions happening less with less budget

- We can do something to **ease** the pain
- Should we **look** at other systems?
- They **saw** the promotional opportunities
- There is **light** at the end of the tunnel
- I've been **hearing** a lot about the new Sunday paper
- A lot of those new directives got **zapped**
- We had a **voice** in the decisions
- I'm **hearing** this person tell me that isn't so
- Do you **see** it or don't you?
- In my **observation**, the time wasn't right
- The first three orders are **bread and butter**, after that it is all **cream**
- The rest of the company didn't **focus** on the same area
- It's just the way things have **fallen out**
- The **sweet taste** of success
- I can **smell the scent** of money

'I wasn't kissing her. I was just whispering in her mouth.'
Groucho Marx

Predicate Exercise 111

Step A:
1. 'A' generates a sentence using predicates from only one of the three main representational systems. (VAK)
2. 'B' mismatches A's predicates while maintaining an appropriate response.

Step B:
1. 'A' repeats the same sentence.
2. 'B' matches A's predicates.

Step C:
1. Repeat Steps A and B, generating sentences, until all three categories with matching predicates have been used.

2. Rotate positions. When each participant has generated sentences using all three systems, move on to Step D.

Step D:
1. 'A' generates a sentence using a 'sequence' of the various predicate systems.
2. 'B' matches the sequence of predicates in their responses.
3. Repeat Step D using a different sequence of the various predicate systems. After three sentences have been accurately completed, change positions.

Record Your Experiences.

What did you experience when the practitioner mismatched the representational system that you were using?

Conversely, what happened when the practitioner matched the representational system you were using?

Group Discussion to Predicate Exercise 111

So what does this mean? How can you use this insight to be a more effective communicator and presenter?

Example 1: The ability to adapt your language to the predicates of others is necessary to form good relationships at work and home. List some of these relationships:

Example 2: To establish rapport quickly, communicate most effectively, and influence a large group, the presenter must communicate in all three sensory channels. List some upcoming presentations and write in the monetary value to you when you win each account:

Add up monetary value when you win all that you listed:

Predicate exercise IV

First person: Describe your dream house or car or holiday, using mostly visual predicates. After four or five sentences . . .

Second person: Pick up the story, but use mostly auditory predicates. After four or five sentences . . .

Third person: Pick up the story using mostly kinaesthetic predicates.

First person: Begin a new story using only auditory predicates.

Second person: Pick up the story using only kinaesthetic predicates.

Third person: Pick up the story using only visual predicates . . . and so on, until each person has had experience using each type of predicate exclusively in several sentences of a story.

Outcome:

Discover which systems are easy for you to generate and which are more difficult. Note that you can access all predicates, depending on your need to express a particular experience.

At a concert you might talk more about the piano's sound rather than what the pianist was wearing (the visual aspect).

With Mick Jagger, though, you might talk in equal predicates about the sight of his energy, the noise of his music, and the excitement of being there—a totally involving experience.

Eye Accessing

Note that eye movements occur when questions re the past are asked.

Accessing Cues (as you face the other person)

Diagram represents generalised human behaviour.

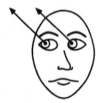  

Up Visual
(Constructed imagery)

Visual—Eyes Defocused
(fixed position usually pupil dilation. Visual imagery remembered or constructed)

Up Visual Eidetic
(Remembered imagery)

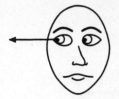

Horizontal Auditory

(Constructed Sound)

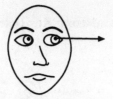

Horizontal Auditory

(Remembered Sound)

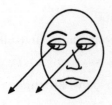

Down Kinaesthetics

(Feelings)

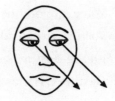

Down
Auditory Tonal

(internal dialogue)

Note: This may be reversed for left-handed people.

Visual representational system

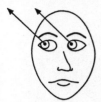 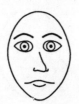 

- Voice: Often high and fast.
- Posture: Neck extended, head tilted up, leans forward.
- Gestures: Up and out. Expansive to draw pictures in the air.
- Breathing: High in chest, shallow, rapid breathing.
- Predicate Language: Look, observe, view, scan, focus, glance, read, colours, watch, visualise, draw, light on, sight, peer, appear, daze, see, get the picture?

Auditory Representational System

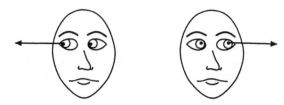

- Voice: Melodious, varied, soft, rhythmic.
- Posture: Head tilted to one side, favours one ear (telephone posture).
- Gestures: Hands near face, mouth, ears, jaw. Rhythmic to mark words.
- Breathing: Relatively deep, middle of chest, even in rate.
- Predicate Language: Say, speak, talk, declare, cry, reporting, utter, express, whisper, announce, hear, listen, tell, discuss, sounds, static, tone, music, in tune with me?

Kinaesthetic Representational System (Feeling/sensation)

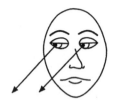

- Voice: Often deep. Words said slowly with pauses.
- Posture: Head and eyes often down. Body may slouch.
- Gestures: Hands folded on stomach or chest. Hand movements low.
- Breathing: Low from the belly and regular.
- Predicate Language: Feel, touch, handle, excited, aroused, reactive, expressive, sense, emotional, anxious, dislike, desire, heavy, deep, walk, joined, active—grasp the idea?

Eye accessing exercise 1

This requires the participation of two people. A reminder that eye movements occur when questions re the past are asked.

Step A:

'A' asks the 'B' the following questions and observes eye movements. A's objective here is to correlate the similarities and differences between the kind of information A is seeking and the non-verbal eye movements of B. If B gives responses which A does not understand, A should ask B what they were thinking.

'The only normal people are the ones you don't know very well.'
Joe Ancis

Visual—Remembered

- How many windows does your house have?
- Where did you sit at home?
- How many pairs of shoes do you own?

Visual—Constructed

- How would you look with green-coloured hair?
- Imagine the house you live in becoming three times larger.

Auditory—Remembered

- Remember something a workmate said this morning.
- Hear the sound of a favourite song.

Auditory—Constructed

- Listen to a train's whistle playing a familiar song.
- What would you say if someone asked you how to eliminate the possibility of Middle East war?

Auditory—Digital—talking to yourself

- Tell yourself what you have to do before you go to bed tonight.

- Tell yourself how you will benefit from this training.

Kinaesthetic—feeling
- How did you feel this morning when you woke up?
- How do you feel after you go for a swim or exercise?

Olfactory/ Gustatory—Smell/Taste
- Remember the smell of a baking cake.
- Remember the taste of your favourite fruit.

Step B: Switch positions and repeat the exercise.

Step C: Make up your own questions to elicit visual, auditory, or kinesthetic responses.

What communicates the message?
A mix of:
- Voice tone
- Words—especially with the understanding of NLP
- Body language
- Voice qualities

Voice Matching exercise I
Step A: 'A' generates two to three sentences exaggerating the voice volume.

Step B: 'B' responds and mismatches the volume of 'A''s voice.

Step C: 'A' continues speaking at same volume for two to three sentences.

Step D: 'B' responds, matching the volume level of A.

Step E: Repeat exercise, varying the rate of speech. Switch roles.

Step F: Complete questions 1 & 2.
1. How would you describe the experience when the practitioner mismatched the volume or tempo of your voice?

2. How would you describe the experience when the practitioner matched the volume or tempo of your voice?

Group discussion on voice matching exercises
  a. What generalisations can you make about voice matching?
  b. How can you use this skill to make you a more effective communicator?

Mirroring

Mirroring is a process used to 'match' your own non-verbal behaviour and vocal tones (i.e. tone, tempo, pitch, and volume, hand gestures, body posture) with that of another person.

By developing the skill necessary to mirror another's communication without it becoming obvious to him or her that you are doing so, you can effect an unconscious sense of trust on the part of that person and thereby establish higher levels of rapport.

Example: A salesperson is approached by a customer upset over an encounter with the head office. The salesperson decides to use the mirroring technique to establish rapport and bring the customer to a more reasonable state of mind.

The salesperson mirrors the rapid tempo of his customer's voice as well as his fast, shallow breathing, and tightly interlaces his fingers in the image of the customer.

After matching the customer's behaviour, the salesperson begins to lead him to a calmer state of mind. He slows his voice tempo, unlocks and relaxes his fingers, and takes a deep breath—all of which the customer may now unconsciously mirror back. The salesperson has established rapport and is creating a relaxed atmosphere in which to resolve the problem.

Mirroring Exercise 1

This exercise requires the participation of a subject, practitioner, and assistant.

Step A: 'A' recalls a past experience that was emotional (i.e. winning a race, the birth of a child, or a roller coaster ride). Go back and re-live the experience as fully as you can.

Step B: 'B' matches the non-verbal aspects of A. Mirror posture, muscle tones, and place of breathing in the chest as closely as you can.

Assistant: Help 'B' match the subject's non-verbals exactly. Maintain this posture for 30–60 seconds and imagine what would be happening to you right now in this body posture and expression. Guess what the subject is thinking. Find out if you are correct.

Step C: Rotate positions until all have had the experience.

Step D: Please record your experience here:

What happened when you matched the subject to this extent and tried to guess their thoughts?

Group discussion on mirroring exercise 1

What conclusions or interpretations can you make about this experience? So what does this mean?

How can this apply in your work to make you more successful with your clients?

Pacing and leading exercise 1

This requires the participation of a subject and practitioner.

Step A: 'B' describes an issue with a client on which they are currently working. Include any objections the client has to what 'B' is selling.

Step B: 'A' roleplays this individual.

Step C: 'B' establishes rapport by mirroring body posture, voice qualities and representational systems. Pay attention to eye accessing if the subject doesn't reveal specific predicates. Once rapport is established, influence the subject to your point of view.

Step D: Rotate positions. Comments about the exercise:

Outcome/Problem Frame
Exercise 1

This exercise requires the participation of a subject and a practitioner.

Step A: 'A' identifies a problem currently being experienced.

Step B: 'B' asks 'A' the following set of questions and writes down the responses.

1. What is the problem?

2. What caused the problem?

3. How is this limiting you?

4. What are the long-term consequences of this situation if
   it continues?

5. Is this a recurring problem?

Step C: 'B' now asks 'A' the following set of questions and
writes in the responses.

1. What are three possible solutions?

a

b

c

2. Which of these do you prefer?

3. What will that do for you?

4. How can you make it happen for you?

5. How can you utilise this obstacle to make you more successful?

6. How will this experience benefit you in the future?

Step D: Switch roles. Record your experiences.

What did you experience when you were asked the first set of questions: What is the problem, what caused the problem?

What happened when you were asked the second set of questions: What do you want? How will you fix the problem?

Group Discussion: Insights/learnings from Exercise 1
In what situations would you want to use questions from the 'problem cause' frame?

In what situations would you want to use questions from the problem solution/outcome frame?

Listening For Criteria /Using Criteria to Influence Criteria exercise

This exercise requires the participation of a subject, practitioner and observer.

Step A: 'A' asks 'B' the following questions. Listen for their criteria (language) and take notes. Observer 'C' does likewise.

Q. Why did you choose to buy your current automobile?

Q. Why did you choose your most recent holiday?

Q. If you were hiring someone to do your job, what personal qualities would you look for?

If you had a free afternoon, with all the money you wanted, how would you spend the time? . . . Why did you choose that activity? What would that do for you?

Step B: Practitioner and Observer plan a presentation to sell the Subject a gizmo/thingummy for $5000.00.

Step C: Practitioner sells the gizmo/thingummy to the Subject using the criteria elicited from the conversation. Exchange places until all have been sold to.

Group Discussion to Exercise: Selling gizmo/thingummy.
How did you feel about selling and buying?

Anchoring Techniques

Definition: Anchoring is the process of attaching a stimulus (V, A or K) to a response.

Anchoring occurs when a specific stimulus, such as a sound, a touch, a smell, a taste or a visual gesture becomes associated with an experience.

The Chinese, for instance, whisper in their child's ear when they are being naughty. Soon the sight of an adult bending down to whisper stops them in their tracks.

Johnny Carson used to anchor his audience with a golf swing. He never had to say, 'Let's go'.

The best time to create an anchor is when rapport is at its highest peak. You can use key words, specially emphasised phrases, smile, point a finger, tap the table, raise your eyebrows or snap your fingers. Then you can bring back that high rapport instantly by using the same verbal or non-verbal cue when the time is right.

To make your anchoring even more effective, try to match your anchor to your client's predominant thinking mode. If your client is visual, use visual anchors like smiling, pointing a finger in the air or nodding your head.

For auditories, you can snap your fingers, clap your hands, tap objects, make your voice strong and excited.

For kinaesthetics, who respond very much to touch, use a pencil or your finger, but keep it to near the elbow. Lower down the arm can be too intimate.

For yourself you can anchor a time when you felt terrific by recalling that time, and pressing your fingernail into your first knuckle. Then anytime you want to recall that time, you simply rub that spot.

Great for going into presentations, before you serve at tennis, facing up to a difficult client or just enjoying life every day.

List examples of anchors that you would feel comfortable with:

Group discussion: In what context could you use anchoring to give you more influence?

Now in your own words, write how you think this NLP training will help you.

_____

_____

Pick out the words you used that express any or all of the languages, and list them here:

V _____

A _____

K _____

O/G _____

KEY POINTS TO REMEMBER

Understand others by understanding yourself. Use your knowledge of personality profiles and neurolinguistics to see, hear and feel what is going on around you.

■ ■ ■

The way forward requires planning. Growth Skill 11 will give you the simplest and most efficient aids (SWOT analysis, business plans, marketing plans and personal business plans) that I could find anywhere in the world.

GROWTH SKILL 11
CREATE POWERFUL BUSINESS MARKETING AND PERSONAL PLANS

'The breakfast of champions is not cereal, it is the opposition.'
Nick Seitz

Now that you have decided on your business and thought your way through the tactical steps to make you successful, it is time to pause and think strategically. Here's how:

STAND IN THE FUTURE AND LOOK BACK TO TODAY

A simple and very effective technique for planning the future for either business or personal needs is to project yourself ahead in your mind's eye and then look back to where you are today.

Pause now, look up from this book and travel to where you want to be in, say, two years. **Act as if you had already achieved these future goals. Feel them, touch them, see them, taste the successes.**

Now look back to where you are today and you will quite clearly see the actions that you put in place to make this future success happen.

To record your action plan, draw a line across a sheet of paper in a shape that expresses how you see your business developing over the coming years. The line could go straight across, indicating your business staying the same, or up (if you are optimistic), or down (if you are pessimistic).

Now draw lines going down on the vertical and fill in your key actions by three-month divisions. Then write in your quarterly activities.

Adjust your current time scales, expenditures, actions and financial program to overcome any obstacles you may encounter in getting from 'here' to 'there'.

When your vision from that future time is consistent with the time, money and actions required to get there, you will be able to move forward with confidence. To see the future and plan for it competently is that simple. When you have done it, you can write your marketing and business (or personal) plans accordingly.

OVERVIEW OF A BUSINESS PLAN

Since many companies don't have an actively used business plan (mostly it seems to be lying at the bottom of a filing cabinet somewhere), and all businesses need one, I now offer an outline and discussion of what I consider a business plan should include.

It is designed to help you to begin the thinking process. Three books are recommended in the reading list at the back under the heading 'Business Plans'.

First you need a SWOT analysis of your business as it stands today, SWOT meaning Strengths, Weaknesses, Opportunities and Threats. In Growth Skill 12, you will read about how various companies identified their needs and then really did something about it.

For instance, with Procter & Gamble and their Pampers product, their strength was that they already had 13 per cent of the disposable diaper market. They were therefore not starting off as a new product trying to enter a crowded market.

When you become a star, you don't change, everybody else does.'
Kirk Douglas

Their weakness was that they were new in the Asian market, and competitive products had the other 87 per cent. The opportunity was to send in a new team and spend money wisely and well (since their budgets were limited). The threat was the other major brand disposable diapers that were competitive in price and quality and had market dominance.

In taking action, the P & G people decided that being market leader with Pampers was the only acceptable position. This was achieved in principle within 14 months. The demand was such that they would have had 52 per cent of the market.

However, the factory could not keep up with this demand. In addition, we found that the product was being diverted from Hong Kong and sold on the black market in Taiwan. Pampers therefore stood at 42 per cent of the market as I left to work in England.

Saatchi & Saatchi/MSL, an executive recruitment company in London, saw their strength as being a well-established, highly reputable company. Their weakness was that they had become complacent and lost market share over the last decade. The opportunity was to retake the high ground and be visible again as market leaders. The threat was in the form of younger, more actively competitive companies who had taken over MSL's position.

The full weight of the skills described in this book was thrown against the problem to the extent that a business associate from Unilever said he had never previously heard of MSL and now was having nightmares about the company!

IMCOR in New York identified their strength as having a new product (interim management/executive leasing) that the marketplace wanted. Their weakness was that they had been relying on networking as their sales process and now realised that they had to expand their reach.

'Your education earns you a living— your self-education earns you a fortune.'
Jim Rohn

'We were running out of friends,' to quote Chairman John Thompson. The opportunity was to become market leader in America, and the threat was the length of time and costs it takes to get a new product up and running profitably.

Five years is usually the minimum time required for that to occur. Again the full weight of the growth skills described in this book was put into play and within 18 months IMCOR had achieved market dominance and profitability. Was it coincidence that this happened about five years after the company had started out in business?

Thomas Cook in Australia had identified their strength as being their highly reputable name in the travel industry, but their weakness was that they had lost their market dominance in cruise bookings.

Also their traditional market of older, English-background clients was dying out. The opportunity was to expand their reach into the younger market, aged 35 and below. The threat was that many other companies were already in touch with the youth market and doing it well.

Realising this, Thomas Cook set out to attract the young market in a way that was highly personal and experiential, such as holding a disco in conjunction with Sitmar cruises. Interestingly, this strategy brought in the parents too and Thomas Cook achieved new dominance in P & O cruises, and Royal Viking cruises as well as Sitmar.

The above SWOT examples are explained more fully towards the back of this book via case studies, and here is one more, on Johnson & Johnson.

Johnson & Johnson USA diversified into another division called Health Management Inc, which offered health facilities from testing units to full-blown gymnasiums fully managed and operated by J & J HMI. Their strength was the parent

'It is really hard to be roommates with people if your suitcases are much better than theirs.'
J.D. Salinger

name, and their product was immediately perceived as trustworthy and value for money.

Their weakness was that their most profitable market consisted of large organisations who wanted the whole lot through to the installation and management of a complete gymnasium, with supervised health and fitness for the thousands of staff they employed. This market was collapsing in on itself with one in three large companies re-forming each year, as opposed to one in ten in the previous decade.

The opportunity was to re-form J & J HMI itself by reviewing their product offerings against the abilities of the remaining corporations to pay, particularly in view of the recessionary times in America. The threats to J & J HMI were:

(1) The competition from other companies also offering in-house health care;

(2) Other gym facilities in which corporations could buy memberships at less than the cost of in-house programs;

(3) The delay in perceivable benefits as early statistics indicated that it took three years for a corporation's bottom line to reflect the increased well-being of its staff (and therefore less time off and fewer industrial accidents). Fewer corporations could now afford to wait that length of time, so the task was to re-form the J & J product to suit this changing market.

Now begin to think through the strengths, weaknesses, opportunities and threats of your own business? I recommend that you do your thinking in the exact SWOT order, beginning with strengths and weaknesses. I have occasionally reversed or shifted the order around to find out what would happen.

If I concentrate on the threats first, for instance, I find myself overly concerned because I am not coming at them from that beginning position of strength. Similarly, I see the opportunities far better if I acknowledge my strengths and weaknesses first. Finally, the threats seem quite small when the other three are in place.

For you to define your key strategic and tactical issues, here is a SWOT analysis that I have used for myself and for clients. It is simple, it works and it also gives you a readout of the culture of your organisation. Since culture is a reflection of what goes on internally, you cannot change or fix the cultural issues unless you change or fix the key strategic and tactical issues.

You will note that you answer 'true' or 'not true' to the statements. If you answer 'true' it is an issue to be discussed and changed; if you answer 'not true' then it is not a problem—it's a positive aspect of your organisation. It's that simple—so go for it!

And when you have decided what your key strategic and tactical issues are, reflect upon them as if they were icebergs. It is only by going around the iceberg, and down into the depths that you can see its full magnitude. Hence the more time you spend analysing what is causing the problems, the quicker you fix the problems at the other end.

Example: A start-up company had grown quickly and the staff had no clear understanding of the purpose and direction of the organisation. This was their key strategic issue. Also they had too many customer complaints because deliveries arrived later than promised. This was their key tactical issue.

The culture of the organisation was that everything was a priority, at the expense of proper planning, so they were reactive rather than proactive.

We realised that the three entrepreneurs who had started

'The advantage of emotions is that they lead us astray.'
**Oscar Wilde
(1854–1900)**

the company had never really talked through their individual visions for the future; they were in such harmony that they didn't need to. But their staff needed to know. To find the words for the strategic purpose and direction, I asked each of the owners to separately write down their key actions for the coming three years.

Then I asked them to give a score out of 10 as to the importance of each activity in the coming three years. The activities were then written up in order of ranking and the staff brought in.

In a matter of minutes they absorbed the work on the blackboard, said, 'Fine,' and moved on to the key tactical issue, which was of course, the customer complaints.

They realised that they had too many customer complaints because they had grown so fast that their systems and procedures were not adequate for the volume of work going through. On the spot they appointed a staff member (with previous experience) to fix their systems and procedures.

An important point relative to working parties for fixing particular problems or opening up new opportunities: never, never go beyond eight people, preferably less.

Why? Think of a dinner party that you went to when there were ten or more people at the table. It split somewhere in the centre and turned into a 'them and us' situation. It is exactly the same at work.

Up to eight people is a functioning entity; after eight you have two separate groups, neither one of which is in communication with the other.

Strange but true. I have a friend who was one of 12 children and he said that they hardly spoke to each other, they were so divided—all of them.

'First secure an independent income, then practice virtue.'
Greek saying

YOUR COMPANY'S STRENGTHS, WEAKNESSES, OPPORTUNITIES AND THREATS (SWOT) ANALYSIS

Use this analysis every three months to see how you are progressing in general terms. Frequent use means that you can track your growth and control and correct your failings.

Use the problem-solving analysis for all weaknesses.

The good news: when you have identified a weakness, simply go to the problem-solving model at the end of the SWOT analysis and use it to define what caused the problem and how to fix it. Then make sure it is fixed.

Start your SWOT here and answer True or Not True

(If it is true, it is a problem and needs fixing; if it is not true, it is a benefit and needs nurturing.)

As Sir Ian MacLennan of BHP in Australia said, 'A good mine is one that produces in spite of its management and the same is true for businesses worldwide.' SWOT analyses are like family analyses: we realise we have problems but we get on okay, in spite of them. But fixing the worst bits is a good idea.

One: The outside world and you

1. Changes are happening outside
    that pose various threats to us.   True   Not True

Whether you answer 'True' or 'Not true', write in what those threats mean to you, in the space below:

And now analyse what the above means to you via the following SWOT spaces.

S. What are your perceived **strengths** from the above issue?

W. What are your perceived **weaknesses** from the above issue?

O. What are the **opportunities** relative to the above issue?

T. What are the **threats** relative to the above issue?

Two: Culture (the internal beliefs and processes of your company)

Note that this section is a reflection only of the strategic and tactical direction of the company, up to and including today. Hence you do NOT analyse the strengths, weaknesses, opportunities and threats here; that analysis belongs in the Strategic and Tactical sections that follow further on.

When you identify a weakness within the following Strategic and Tactical sections, you need only to reverse the behaviour or fix the problem, for the culture to change.

Continue to mark True or Not True to all the following.

a. The future:

1. We are not very optimistic
   about the future   True   Not True

b. In our workday it seems that:

1. We are short-term, oriented
   in our behaviours   True   Not True

2. We react to circumstances
   rather than trying to foresee
   and control them   True   Not True

3. We seem to be solving past
   problems more than getting
   on with current and future
   client needs   True   Not True

'No matter what goes wrong, it will probably look right.' **Scott's First Law**

c. Getting things done:

1. Too much paperwork and
   procedures   True   Not True

2. And too many managers,
   not enough action   True   Not True

d. Growing as people:

1. We don't feel that we are being
   challenged to do our best   True   Not True

2. We don't really stretch ourselves to achieve the company's
   goals, as we know them   True   Not True

e. Staff interaction and performance:

1.	It is more important to be popular than to achieve results	True	Not True
2.	We accept anything that is reasonably okay	True	Not True
3.	Risk taking is not encouraged	True	Not True
4.	Creativity is not encouraged	True	Not True
5.	We are not encouraged to try new things, even if we make mistakes	True	Not True

f. Senior management support:

1.	Key managers are not able to support change	True	Not True

g: Internal self-management:

1.	We don't discuss the really difficult issues	True	Not True
2.	Too many excuses, not enough action	True	Not True
3.	Problems remain unsolved because we don't speak out or fix them when we do speak out	True	Not True
4.	We don't respect each other enough	True	Not True

'When an error has been detected and corrected, it will be found to have been correct in the first place.'
Scott's Second Law

h. As a result there can be:

1.	Face-to-face arguments	True	Not True
2.	Behind-their-back remarks of an unkind nature	True	Not True
3.	Too much time fighting/blaming one another	True	Not True

i. In team work we believe there is:

1. Insufficient teamwork between
    top and middle management   True   Not True

2. And departments argue against
    departments resulting in a
    we/they attitude   True   Not True

Now for your key strategic issues:

(This is where you find out the influences that are shaping the culture of your company or business, and what you need to reverse or change to improve the way your business operates. Here is where you conduct your analysis, using the SWOT spaces below.)

Three: Looking at leadership

1. Management is not in control
    of the organisation   True   Not True

2. Management seeks growth at the
    expense of profit   True   Not True

3. Management seeks sales at the
    expense of profit   True   Not True

4. Targets are set that we don't feel
    we can achieve   True   Not True

5. Everything is urgent and has to
    be done now   True   Not True

6. We are doing too many different
    things at the same time   True   Not True

7. We are not sure what the
    company's goals are   True   Not True

'Nothing succeeds like the appearance of success.'
Christopher Lasch

Now analyse your findings via this SWOT section.

Note: Your strengths will be those that you marked as 'Not

True' and your weaknesses those you marked as 'True'. Opportunities will be those that you now see from your answers, as will threats.

S _____

_____

W _____

_____

O _____

_____

T _____

_____

Four: How you see your company as being structured

1. The way the business is currently organised does not help us meet our goals   True   Not True

2. People are more important than the goals set   True   Not True

3. One or two key people make the big decisions   True   Not True

4. We are not involved in the future
   plans and decisions   True   Not True
5. We conduct too many unproductive
   meetings   True   Not True
6. There is too much management
   by committee   True   Not True
7. We are not asked to voice
   problems, concerns and opinions True   Not True
8. We do not develop enough new
   ideas for our clients and prospects True   Not True

Your analysis from your answers above:

S

W

O

T

Five: The way we are rewarded

1. The way we are paid does not
   encourage us to reach the
   company's goals   True   Not True

Your analysis from your answer above:

S
_____
_____

W
_____
_____

O
_____
_____

T
_____
_____

Now for your key tactical issues:

Here you learn more about the behaviours of your company
and what needs to change to be more successful—thereby
changing the company culture. More analysis is required
using the SWOT spaces at the end of each section.

Six: You and your competition, customers and prospects

1. We don't worry enough about our
   competition   True   Not true

2. We are at the mercy of our systems
   rather than market-driven   True   Not True

3. We are not really focused on
   client satisfaction   True   Not True

4. We are not trained to know how
   our performance affects the
   customer's sense of quality
   and satisfaction   True   Not True

5. We do not have clear definitions
   of customer-defined quality and
   service   True   Not True

Your analysis from your answers above:

S

W

O

T

Seven: Your business, its tactics

1. We rely on too few key
   customers   True   Not True
2. We do not understand our
   marketing plan   True   Not True
3. We do not know if we are
   correctly positioned in our
   market   True   Not True
4. Our prices/fees are too high
   compared to our competition   True   Not True
5. We do not adequately promote
   our business and all that it offers   True   Not True
6. We are not satisfied with our
   corporate image and identity   True   Not True

Your analysis from your answers above:

S

W

O

T

Eight: Space to work in, equipment and systems to work with

1.	We are growing too fast for our space	True	Not True
2.	We struggle with outdated technology	True	Not True
3.	We have too many procedures and policies	True	Not True
4.	We don't follow our procedures and policies	True	Not True
5.	Our workflow could be more efficient	True	Not True
6.	Our accounting systems could be more efficient	True	Not True

Your analysis from your answers above:

S

W _____

O _____

T _____

Nine: People—hiring, evaluating, training

1. We are short-staffed most of the
   time   True   Not True
2. We are not good at selecting
   effective people   True   Not True
3. You can get away with being
   incompetent   True   Not True
4. Performance is rarely if ever
   evaluated effectively   True   Not True
5. We keep low-performing people on,
   rather than make waves   True   Not True
6. People have to learn as they go,
   without proper induction and
   training   True   Not True
7. We do not have a sense of being
   developed for management or
   other career paths   True   Not True

8. Company management cannot cope with the current demands of the job   True   Not True

9. Too many people not contributing   True   Not True

10. Too many people in the wrong jobs   True   Not True

11. We are missing some supervisory and management skills in key positions   True   Not True

Your analysis from your answers above:

S

W

O

T

Ten: At the end of the day

(This is where you get an overall picture of your company. On the way through the earlier statements, it may seem to you that there are a lot of difficult issues. When we do this section though, it may then seem that there are only a few key issues after all.)

1.	We sometimes make too many mistakes	True	Not True
2.	We are up and down in our relationships internally and with clients	True	Not True
3.	We achieve little in real terms on a daily basis	True	Not True
4.	We have low morale	True	Not True
5.	Some of our staff are already burnt out	True	Not True
6.	Some of our customers complain too much	True	Not True
7.	Other similar businesses are more competitive than we are	True	Not True
8.	Our financial management is inadequate	True	Not True
9.	We lose too many valued clients	True	Not true
10.	We lose too many clients overall	True	Not True
11.	We don't know why we lose clients	True	Not True
12.	We don't get in enough new clients	True	Not True
13.	Our clients seem bored with our product/service	True	Not True
14.	We market inefficiently and without consistency	True	Not True

'At the end of the day' analysis from your answers.

S _____

_____

W _____

_____

O _____

_____

T _____

_____

Now write in your key issues from this analysis (the Strategic sections 3–5 and the Tactical sections 6–9, nominating those which your 'gut feeling' tells you are the most important.

Strengths
Strategic: go to your notes in sections 3–5 and choose those issues of key importance, by your gut feeling. (Remember that these strategic strengths will always be found in the statements marked 'Not True'.)

Write down those issue in the box below.

Strengths
Tactical: go to sections 6–9 and choose those issues of key importance, by your gut feeling. (Remember that these tactical strengths will always be found in the statements marked 'Not True'.)

Weaknesses
Strategic: go to your notes in sections 3–5 and choose those issues of key importance, by your gut feeling. (Remember that these strategic weaknesses will always be found in the statements marked 'True'.)

Weaknesses
Tactical: go back to sections 6–9 and choose those issues of key importance, by your gut feeling. (Remember that these

tactical weaknesses will always be found in the statements marked 'True'.)

Opportunities

Strategic: go back again to sections 3–5. Go back through your notes in the SWOT analysis and choose those issues of key importance.

Opportunities

Tactical: go back again to sections 6–9. Go back through your notes in the SWOT analysis and choose those issues of key importance.

Threats

Strategic: return once more to sections 3–5. Go back through your notes in the SWOT analysis and choose those issues of key importance.

Write down those issues in the box below.

Threats

Tactical: return to sections 6–9. Go through your notes in the SWOT analysis and choose the issues of key importance.

At the end of the day

Nominate your key issues from section 10, at the end of the day, working on your gut feeling.

Strengths (from 'Not True')

Weaknesses (from 'True')

Opportunities (from those decided on by gut feeling from your notes.)

_____

_____

Threats (from those decided on by gut feeling from your notes)

_____

_____

Combine your findings in a report on your overall strengths, weaknesses, opportunities and threats, and use the following problem-solving model to solve any and every problem you may have, be it personal or business.

Now for your problem-solving of your weaknesses

Disregard for the moment the weaknesses from the 'culture' section, as culture is only a reflection of the strategic and tactical direction imposed on the business, up to and including today.

Instead look at the weaknesses in the strategic and tactical sections and work on those. The culture of your business will change as the weaknesses are reversed.

Here is the problem-solving model to help you make those changes. This exercise works well with a partner, similarly involved in the business. Hence I have nominated an A and a B. But you can do it on your own if you have no likely person to work with you.

You, being A, identify in a few words a problem you are currently experiencing from the SWOT analysis. Now B asks you the following questions and writes down the responses.

1. What is the problem? (If from the SWOT analysis, write in the exact words, or as you have redefined it.)

2. What caused the problem?

3. How is this limiting you?

4. What are the long-term consequences of this situation if it continues?

5. Is this a recurring problem?

_____

_____

B now asks A the following set of questions and writes in the responses.

1. What are three possible solutions?

a _____

b _____

c _____

2. Which of these do you prefer?

_____

_____

_____

3. What will that do for you?

_____

_____

_____

4. How can you make it happen for you?

_____

_____

5. How can you use this obstacle to become more successful?

_____

_____

Now take whatever action is needed to ensure a result, which may include developing a working party of no more than eight people, and preferably less, to truly identify the levels of the problem, and how best to fix it.

PS: Use the above problem-solving model anywhere, anytime you or someone else has a problem. Bring solutions to the table, not complaints.

YOUR BUSINESS PLAN

Now that you have done your SWOT analysis, you are ready for your strategic and tactical business plan.

Key issue: There are three 'musts' to having a successful company. You must have:

- Good product
- Good marketing
- Good financial management.

If any one of these three is missing, your business will fail.

Please first read through this whole section before doing

any planning, so that you get a clear understanding of what planning is all about and why you are doing it.

Be realistic, congruent and relevant

It is important to put your wants into a congruent flow so that each enhances the other. For instance, say you are a company making children's toys. You want to increase profit by 15 per cent per annum over the next three years. You can do it by either cutting costs or expanding your sales profitably.

Let's say you choose to cut costs by cutting back staffing, year one. However, you want to increase your Research & Development division so that you will be prepared for the next toy-selling season. And you want to improve customer service and production quality because your research shows you're seen as unhelpful with complaints—of which you have too many.

Now you have two plans which call for increased staff and facilities, pulling against the plan to cut staff. Your decision to increase profit by 15 per cent will die on the vine.

Let's say you decide to expand profitably instead. If you are absolute market leader in your field, you are the benchmark for all other similar companies. If, however, you are below that first position, your key question is: where do you now lie, relative to your competition? You need to know in order to verify your belief that you can achieve an increase of 15 per cent per annum over the years of your business plan.

First work out the industry norm for increase in sales. Look at total sales of all similar companies (adjusted for inflation) over the past three years. Did you increase your sales more/less/the same in comparison? If more, was it sufficient to make you feel secure about achieving your 15 per cent increase?

If the industry norm has been a 10 per cent increase over the past few years and you have achieved that also, there is not a great deal of reason to think you can reach an increase of 15 per cent without considerable expenditure of, say, time and money in customer service, staff training and better product, sales force, packaging, response time, distribution, advertising and promotional activities, plus tighter financial controls.

If, however, you find an industry norm of 15 per cent and you have not achieved it, it is time to look at why, before you make any plans for the future.

It can be that you used to achieve industry norm or even beyond in growth, but you have changed as an organisation and have moved from a shooting star, high in activity and excitement, and low in cash, to a sort of middle-aged spread, where you have no real competitive advantage any more, but are just one of many struggling to make a living.

'Learn to help people with more than just their jobs; help them with their lives.'
Jim Rohn

In that case you have to find a whole new way of looking at your business plan. What is it that you want for your company relative to the truth as you now see it?

Could you occupy a niche supplying educational toys by catalogue to parents anxious to entertain and educate their children other than with TV?

How would this impact on your current systems? Could it be done cost-effectively or would you go broke in making all the changes long before the product had a chance of making money?

Who is your purchaser?

Key issue: After people see something they like, they buy from greed, fear and laziness. Are you meeting all three in your selling process?

Another good question is: does anyone really want my product? Is there so much competition around that people buy what they see, rather than by brand? Will your product be overtaken by cheaper overseas imports? Could you manufacture overseas and distribute from there more cheaply and effectively, thereby ridding yourself of the complaints problem?

What is your market share? A simple mathematical process will tell you. You divide your annual sales by that of the total industry sales of similar companies. If you sold $1000 of toys and the total industry sales were $1,000,000, you would have 0.001 per cent market share (according to my calculator).

Your relative market share is also interesting. To find this out you divide your sales for the year by that of your nearest competitor. If you did $1000 and they did $2000, your relative market share is 50 per cent; if they did only $1500 it is 66 per cent. Have you been growing faster than your competitor or falling behind?

If you are a service organisation, ask yourself: does your marketplace really need another recruitment company, another firm of management consultants, another accounting or law firm, another travel agent, another restaurant? What is their industry norm for sales growth over the past three years? Where do you stand? How can you differentiate yourself and what therefore should be your approach to your business plan?

'The enemy came. He was beaten. I am tired. Goodnight.'
Message sent by Vicomte Turenne after the battle of Dunen, 1658

Since you can only grow by taking on more clients and customers or more business from existing clients (and if you do not grow, you go backwards), then your business plan must be about increasing staff and facilities in order to increase business and taking a realistic approach to recouping those costs. Clients and prospects do not read your business plans, they simply do what they want, when they want.

Where do you need to be in the future?

If you decide to contract or expand your staffing, you may want to create a small, efficient task force to move you out of where you are now to where you want to be in the time scale you have chosen. Your present staff may change in numbers and/or in style and qualifications. An accounting firm that decides to focus on an ethnic group may seek people of that race or nationality to work with clients.

A legal firm specialising in immigration from third-world countries may seek people who have spent time in these areas. A management consultancy may decide to focus on the tourist industry and hire people from airlines, hotels, shipping lines, and travel agencies.

All the while it must be acknowledged that the return on the investment will take a long time coming. Which brings us to capital. Realistically, how much money will you need for these changes to take place and return a profit? Over years of doing budgets where many variables are involved, I have found one unchanging rule: whatever budget you set, it always costs twice as much. This seems to apply to personal budgets as well as business ones. The key question is, can you afford the plans you have for the future?

Research your existing client base

Research your existing client base and ask what they think of your organisation, what they consider you provide and how they think you can adapt or grow for the future.

One of the world's favourite stories is about the railroad companies that thought they ran trains up and down lines. To the rest of the world they provided a mode of transport. While the train companies stuck to their knitting (so to speak), other transport opportunities passed them by, as did their passengers.

You need to know whether your clients love you or are staying with you until a better offer comes along. Clients are fickle and will move for almost any reason, including a better price.

For instance, I ran a very successful series of travel supplements in all the major newspapers with free gifts and prizes and great holiday offers from Thomas Cook. The day that promotion finished, another travel company came out with some more good offers. My client's outlets emptied as the others filled.

'Almost anything is easier to get into than to get out of.'
Allen's Law

Absolutely no loyalty! But why should there be when almost all travel shops provide the same range of products? The same is true of a lot of other companies.

The changing needs of your clients and how you respond to them can have a lot to do with government legislation and regulations. If the client cannot understand the new rules on superannuation, for instance, and you can, you have a captive market, but only if you can explain it in a way that we confused buyers can understand. Otherwise, we still feel doubtful and confused.

You now know about your sales volume, growth rate and market share at this time and have thought about what these must be to meet your future plans. 'Adapt or die' is a fair statement at this stage because whatever your expansion plans, you have to have the systems, processes and trained people to make them happen.

Recently I talked with a large retailer about a test market for data collection and lifestyle marketing programs. In conversation with the MIS department I found they are well set up to handle the information flow except that they are also on an acquisition program and about the time the test would be ready to go national, they may well have run out of spare mainframe capacity.

We started out talking about the business plan for introducing database marketing; now we were talking about major costs in systems. Will the database marketing program return sufficient funds to cover these costs in two, three, five years or never? Will the company want to take that risk along with the cost of the acquisitions?

'Any simple idea will be worded in the most complicated way.'
Malek's Law

Action and reaction. However realistic and congruent your plans are, you have to have the people, processes, systems and training to make it work, as well as the capital.

How well is your product or service promoted?

Next, how well is your product or service promoted to the buying public? Do you have a 'single-minded proposition' which quite simply states what you provide from the customer's point of view? (This subject of the single-minded proposition is covered fully in Growth Skill 4.)

For instance, in one case we thought of a timber and hardware company as being 'doctors' to the building and DIY trade, prescribing the best products for the job at hand. If proven, this could then translate to a tag line, 'Building better communities with care'.

This kind of tag line, while not researched and given here as a discussion point only, does show how all their communications to the trade or the consumer—in direct marketing, sales promotion, catalogue sales or public relations—could have a single-minded focus, simply because that one statement was the umbrella under which everything else could hang.

When you come up with that knowledge of how you benefit the buyer and use it to create a tag line for all your communications, you can then decide whether or not you have top-quality advertising, sales promotion, direct marketing, public relations and community relations by comparing your profit **pre** and **post** the use of this discipline.

There will be many other factors that affect your profit, but having clear, simple-minded communications takes you way out in front of the muddled ways of most of your competitors.

Care for the environment

Now for community affairs. 'Am I contributing to the environment or taking away?' is one of the most critical issues in our plans for the coming decades.

Recent research shows that at the top of people's concerns are unemployment and the environment, nominated by around 70 per cent of people interviewed. All other issues were around 20 per cent. So what do we care about in corporate life? We care about the environment because if we don't, we may well be boycotted out of business.

People rightly believe that the world is running out of the capacity to heal itself, while we humans do not have the capacity to adapt well to increasing pollution. So we have to solve the problem. In your business plan, look very carefully at this responsibility even if it seems at first that you can't do much.

If everyone cleaned up their back and front yards, for instance, we would clean up the world. Think of the miracle of the Sydney Harbour clean-up. It led to 'Clean Up Australia' and beyond to the world level. It can be done. It should—it must—be part of everyone's plan for the future.

'Orthodox medicine has not found an answer to your complaint. However, luckily for you, I happen to be a quack.' **Richter cartoon caption**

We want healthy people in our communities who will need our products and services. Sick people have entirely different needs and most of us are not basing our future on being part of the hospital and medical professions. If we make the difference now, we will have clients for the future.

Other government legislation—on equal opportunity, sexual harassment, smoking in the workplace, staff health care, the rights of part-time workers, paternity and maternity leave and superannuation—requires specialist knowledge. Seek it out, get different opinions, attend seminars and make judgements based on sound information.

Training is important and probably the greatest problem

faced by corporations today is how to evaluate programs and their effectiveness. Training organisations all over the world have public seminars so that one or two people can attend before you decide to have a specially focused in-house program. The public trainers are rated after every performance and any bad rating is discussed. Therefore only the good ones survive.

Evaluating effectiveness after training can be as simple as deciding what needs to be fixed, getting it fixed and then seeing if it remains fixed. In my experience, our peer group and immediate managers are the best judges of whether our improvement is ongoing.

'He who hesitates is probably right.' **Bogovich's Law**

Your vision for the future

And now for a vision statement. I remember sitting in Procter & Gamble's office in Hong Kong reading their vision statement, which included giving people the right environment to grow in, to express truth fearlessly, to stand up for what is right and to expect a fair hearing for their opinions, while producing the finest quality products for their customers.

The meeting progressed entirely along those lines. We expected and received a fair hearing for our opinions. As for their products, P & G does have an awesome reputation for product purity. Their vision statement represented their attitude to their customers and to their staff.

Your vision statement should be broad enough to allow for expansion and precise enough for all staff members to feel that they can be part of it.

It is fair to say that if the staff have a say in the vision statement and the business plan, you will get more realistic and congruent objectives than you could achieve in isolation or in a small ivory-tower group.

Say you were a restaurant owner and you chose six to eight

words or phrases to describe your business, now and for the future. You might have noticed that you have and want to continue to have, 'friendly staff, fair prices, great service, great food, clean workplace'.

Then your vision statement in terms of what you plan to do for your customers might become: 'We provide and will continue to provide fine quality food at very fair prices, having constant regard for the highest standards of service and cleanliness and concern for the environment.'

This could mean that you serve only fresh seasonal foods to get the highest quality and the fairest prices, that your staff are hired away from the Regent Hotels and that they and your kitchen are scrubbed pristine clean.

> 'I've known what it is to be hungry, but I always went right to a restaurant.'
> **Ring Lardner**
> **(1885–1933)**

You also use biodegradable washing powders and recycled paper products if you are convinced that the chemicals in recycling do less harm than chopping down renewable trees.

'Providing food' is broad enough to allow for expansion into boardroom catering, special event catering, airport and airline food, staff cafeterias for major business buildings and meals for workers on special projects.

You could go on to children's parties and theme restaurants such as great eateries for truck drivers . . . the list is endless. The choice is yours because your vision is focused but flexible.

NOW FOR YOUR BUSINESS PLAN

To begin your strategic business plan, ask yourself: what is a truly relevant date to plan towards?

Your product cycle may be such that three years is a relevant business plan analysis for you. Five, 10 or 15 years may be better if you are building fleets of container ships or satellites, all the while remembering that constant revision of your business plan is necessary.

1. What is my business about today? (Write today's date in here.....................and describe your business now.)

2. Stand in the future and see it, touch it, feel it; look back to today and ask, 'What do I want for my business by the future date that I am looking back from?' (Write that future date here ....and describe those developments.)

3. How do we get from the present to the future? In its barest bones a business plan has three elements: land, labour and capital. The next step is to analyse these three:

   a. Where is my business physically situated now?

   b. Where should it be in this future time?

c. Who do I have working with me now?

d. How would this change for the future?

e. How am I doing for money now?

f. How much will I need to get to the future?

4. The next key issue is developing your product or service through understanding the customers' needs:

    What am I producing now?

5. What do my clients think of this product/service?

6. How must I improve the product/service and its production to still be in business by my chosen time?

7. What is my sales volume/growth rate/market share now?

8. What must my sales volume/growth rate/market share be in this forward time to make a satisfactory profit which allows for product improvement, price reduction, or greater spending on advertising and promotion? (Otherwise a cheaper competitor will come into your market.)

9. What systems, processes, special training must I put in place to reach that objective?

10. And next, how well is my product/service promoted to the buying market?

11. How well do I express in my sales/marketing and advertising activities what it is that is unique about my product? (Write in here your 'single-minded' proposition—see Growth Skill 4. Try to do it in 12 words or less.)

Now write down an suitable tag line that would follow from the single-minded proposition (see Growth Skill 4).

12. Am I now doing top-quality:

Client/prospect relations?	Yes	No
Advertising?	Yes	No
Direct marketing?	Yes	No
Sales promotion?	Yes	No
Public relations?	Yes	No

Staff relations?	Yes	No
Community relations?	Yes	No
Trade shows?	Yes	No

Your comments:

13. In making decisions about your advertising and promotion, the following received wisdoms are here to assist you in allocating your money and activities. As you promote your products, you will find that different media give different results, such as:

    • Radio advertising brings in brand new customers; print and TV advertising help move clients and customers from your competition; direct marketing builds customer loyalty.

    Plus:

    • You have to spend money in order to be noticed. About half of what you spend will keep you 'top of mind' with your existing client base, the other half will attract new purchasers.

    • Shout, don't whisper. One small advertisement will be lost in the clutter, whereas one big one or 12 little ones, page by page, will call out loudly for attention.

    • The big spend comes first. When you have cut through the clutter of your competitors' advertising and promotional activities, you can reduce your spending considerably, to one-quarter or one-half.

    • Use more than one medium at a time. Print or TV plus

radio will return you up to 50 per cent more responses when they are used together rather than separately.

- Don't struggle for the perfect advertising campaign at the expense of missing your deadline. Good is better, but getting out there is best.

- Most of all, it doesn't matter what you do so long as you get out there and do something. If you smile in the dark, no one can see you. If you smile in the light, the world can smile with you. Don't sit behind closed doors, fearing failure and rejection. Get out there and do something that people can notice and respond to.

- Above all, be different from your competition. If you match their advertising expenditure and use the same media, have the same special offers, look the same, sound the same, you will disappear into their image, not create your own.

Ask yourself, using these guidelines, how should I improve/expand these communication processes to meet my future goals?

14. Community affairs are also a key issue, such as: am I contributing to the earth's environment or taking away?

And how can I be ready for/ahead of government legislation on this and other issues such as equal opportunity, sexual harassment*, smoking in the workplace and staff healthcare, superannuation, paternity and maternity leave, training levy, etc.?

*The best and simplest guideline I have come across for staff on the sexual harassment issue is this: ask yourself if you would like to:

    (a) hear your words repeated on radio

    (b) see your actions replayed on television

    (c) have your family walk in on you at this time

    (d) behave the same way in a place of worship.

If the answer is 'No!' to any of these questions, then it is sexual harassment.

15. Training for now and the future: Are my staff trained in a planned and coordinated way that is relevant to their and my needs? Or is the training largely haphazard? Or non-existent?

What must I therefore put in place to guarantee the training which is required for my future plans to work?

16. Now comes a simple vision statement for the future as to what you plan to provide to the client or customer and how well you are going to do it. First write down about six words that describe your service or product now and then as you want it to be in the future, for your staff and clients/customers.

Next put those words together in a sentence that is clear to you, your staff and the people who buy from you.

Publish thousands of cards with that vision statement on it. Ask your clients to mark 'yes' or 'no' beside the question, 'Did we match our vision statement in our relationship with you?'

Use these cards as market research. Ask for the client's name and phone number on the card and contact each one to ask what was good or not good about your relationship. Learn how to do better as you go—before it is too late.

It may be timely here to mention the definition of quality service: it is simply doing what you say you will do, within the time stated.

Key issue: there are only three ways to grow your company. Grow your client base, grow your profit, grow the frequency of purchase. Are you sufficiently skilled to do all three?

Now that your business plan is complete, move on to your marketing plan.

OUTLINE OF A MARKETING PLAN

'They say you can't do it, but sometimes it doesn't always work.'
Casey Stengel (1891–1975)

You need a marketing plan to follow for the development of sales of your products or services.

I am delighted to recommend to you the following marketing plan revised from **Marketing Without Mystery—a Practical Guide to Writing a Marketing Plan**, Amacom, 1991, by Laura M. Dirks and Sally H. Daniels. Buy this book, it is excellent.

Here is a short form as a practise run, but to be truly effective you should work from the book.

Start first with:

1. Background and objectives:

    A brief statement of background information about your company and what you provide.

- The reasons you are writing this plan and the period of time that it will cover.

- The specific maximum and minimum objectives of the plan (so that you can measure success as you go along).

- An agreed vision statement as to what you will provide your customers and staff during this marketing plan.

2. Who your likely buyers are:
   - A brief description of the people/companies that will buy from you.

- Their needs that your product/service and this plan will serve.

_____

_____

_____

3. Who the competition is and how well it performs:
List your competition, both direct and indirect.

For instance, a travel company may have a direct competitor next door but all other phone and internet booking processes are an indirect competitor, because clients can book direct and bypass you.

- How well that direct and indirect competition serves (or otherwise) this market.

_____

_____

_____

- How your direct competition may react to your business and marketing plans.

_____

_____

_____

- How your indirect competition may react.

_____

4. Promotional activities that you plan to use such as:
   - Publicity/PR—if you do not have the skills in-house, hire a good PR firm.

_____

   - Direct/database marketing—again, hire a good firm if you do not have the skills.

_____

   - Advertising: go with the best advertising agency you can find. They all charge about the same! Remember, a great client makes a great agency, not the other way round.

     Make your advertising agency your business partner. Be there for brainstorming sessions, help them see the whole picture by sharing your goals, your business plans, your marketing plans, your results.

Like doctors, they can't help you effectively until they know the whole picture.

_____

_____

- Personal selling: what this book is all about. Stay within the three-month cycle. Make contact regularly and relentlessly and never fail to follow up.

_____

_____

- Telemarketing for appointments or sale of your product, with a free-phone response number.

_____

_____

- Special events in the areas where your likely buyers can most easily respond.

_____

_____

- Mobile offices for these special events.

- Showroom or quiet viewing area.

- Incentives such as free gift with purchase, two for the price of one.

- Visuals. Under each of these headings write out an analysis of what you are likely to need. For instance Direct Marketing might include:

Well-designed corporate ID

Data entry costs

Brochures and flyers

Mailing lists

Letters using your corporation's ID (see Growth Skill 5)

Newsletters

Media kits

Industry kits

Invitations

Faxes

_____

_____

Phone calls

_____

_____

And envelopes

_____

_____

Envelopes take time to print and should be ordered first. I speak from experience. I cannot tell you the number of times everything has been ready except the envelopes.

The envelopes must have your full name and address on them so that the returns come back to you and you can then clean up your mailing list. Write your one-sentence vision statement on the envelope, under your address, to enhance the reader's understanding of your company.

Contact your local Post Office and get their advice on what is required on the envelope in order to get bulk mailing discounts. You can save quite a lot of money if you are doing big mailings.

Further visuals could include:

Business card

Signs

Training materials

Videos

Name tags

Booklets of promotional photos and information

Folder covers

Banners

Directional signs

These would be designed to integrate well with the items required for direct marketing, for example, and with your advertising.

5. Action plans:
   • Specific tasks (who is going to do what)

   • Dates/times/locations for completion

- Budgets (from which budgets? over what period of time?)

- Assignment of task responsibility overall and authority to sign/approve

6. Agreed measurement guidelines and review dates for whether or not you and your staff and agencies have:
   - Achieved the minimum and maximum objectives as stated in your 'Introduction'

- Contribution to the attainment of the agreed goals   Yes   No

If these have not been achieved, ask how the situation can be fixed. The great advantage of this plan is that everyone knows who is responsible for what, by what time, who has to sign for expenditures and what the minimum and maximum goals are.

The plan can serve as an evaluation process for staff and consulting agencies and can identify areas where training or support is needed. Be flexible, but at the same time firm. If anyone is falling behind in activities, it pulls everyone down.

I have used this type of work analysis for numerous projects, particularly when one or more companies are involved with my client, such as in a joint promotion. The process has ensured successful completion of the marketing effort because each activity had beside it the person to do it and the time to complete it.

At working-group meetings it was easy to identify those who were and those who were not keeping up with the pace. The problem could be fixed accordingly. Be sure to convert your marketing plan to a work-in-progress plan and, by so doing, keep everyone up to the mark.

Here is an example of the beginning of a work-in-progress plan. The detail is minute, but all promotions are made up of many minor details before the big one comes together.

PROMOTE EVENING CONCERTS AT THE ZOO

Key Actions	By (person)	Date
Agree concert content	Director/PR	Jan 20
Agree costs	Director/PR	Jan 20
Book orchestra/singers, etc	PR	Jan 21
Allocate funds	Director	Feb 1
Re-confirm orchestra availability	PR	Feb 2
Develop and sign contract	PR/Director	Feb 20
Pay deposit	Director	Feb 27
Plan staffing levels	Food/Bev Mgr.	Mar 3
Plan catering requirements	' ' '	
Plan public requirements (seating, security, car parking, first aid . . .)	Security	Mar 3
Prepare master plan (Expand and re-write as necessary)	All	April 6

KEY POINTS OF YOUR BUSINESS AND MARKETING PLANS

- Be realistic, go with the truth. If times are tough out there, plan for that. If times are good, put funds away for when the tough times come again, as they always do.
- Be congruent. Make sure your plans pull together in a timely way to common and realistic goals.
- Be relevant. Constantly research your clients and prospects for their changing needs and meet those needs before your competitors do.
- Involve all your staff in your business and marketing plans. They know so much that you need to know but they may not tell you until you ask. Convert your marketing plan to a work-in-progress plan and meet weekly or even daily to keep everyone up to the pace required to perform on time.
- Be flexible. Change your business and marketing plans as the world changes around you. Do not wait or be 'too busy' to see the future. Read widely, attend seminars and conferences. Learn from specialists.
- Set up a personally chosen Board of Advisers to update you monthly on key issues, from changes in government legislation locally to changes in society nationally and internationally.

'O Lord, help me to be perfect, but not yet.'
St Augustine (354–430) (Slightly misquoted)

Your business plans: make this 'standing forward and looking back' work for you.

A reminder: if you have trouble standing forward and looking back to today, draw a line in a shape that expresses how you see your business developing over the number of years you have chosen. Project yourself into the future, own your future! Look back at yourself where you are seated reading these words. You will see quite clearly the key actions that you have to put in place to reach that goal.

Write down the goals that you want to have achieved by those specific times you have chosen. Use as few words as possible, because this will be your personal inner-pocket check-list that you will carry with you everywhere.

Write down the actions that you now know you will need to put in place in order to meet those goals for each specific time. Again, as few words as possible, because they will have to fit on that same list.

Write down the amount of money each goal will cost you. Add that to your list so that every time you are tempted to spend money unnecessarily, you can look at it and ask yourself how much that expenditure will interfere with your future plans.

Make up that check-list in such a way that it can go inside a pocket or a briefcase. Copy a spare one for the glove compartment of your car and another for inside your chequebook or with your credit cards. Still another will be for beside the bed at night. Remind yourself each day of these goals.

In the reading list at the back of this book are three recommendations under the heading 'Business Plans'. If you are serious about a good business plan and one that will work for you and your staff, top to bottom, I feel that you will enjoy and value all of these books.

YOUR PERSONAL BUSINESS PLAN

Here is a personal plan outline for you to use if you would like to see the future for yourself as well as for your business. Since the person who goes to work is also the same person who goes home at night, doing congruent plans for both may appeal to you.

As with your business plan, a very effective technique for

planning your personal needs is to project yourself ahead in your mind's eye and then look back to 'where you are today'.

Again, draw a line as to how you see your life developing: up, for moving into new realms; straight across, for remaining the same; down, if you are feeling that way. If you do draw a down line, try to use this personal business plan to identify how you can make it go across at least, or preferably up.

Pause now and mentally travel two years and then five years ahead (or whatever suits you). Project yourself back to where you are at this moment.

Decide what it is you will have achieved by those times, what actions you will have taken to get there, what kind of income you will have needed to generate. Mentally adjust your current expenditures, actions and future financial program to overcome any obstacles you may encounter in getting from 'here' to 'there'.

How much money do you need to earn to reach your goals?

Now take a few minutes to work out the net income you will require in those future years. I am suggesting a two-year and five-year plan, but alter to whatever suits you.

'I have enough money to last me the rest of my life unless I buy something.'
Jackie Mason

Income package value	+ 2 yrs	+5 yrs
Gross before taxes per annum	$	$ ....
Net after taxes per annum	$	$ ....
Net per week	$	$ ....
Net per hour	$	$ ....

The value of knowing this net-per-hour amount is that every time you waste an hour, or someone wastes an hour for you, you realise that you have thrown away that amount of money and you can only get it back by working unpaid overtime.

Now to your personal plan: start with the end in mind. Look at this day and ask yourself:

1. What is my personal life like at this time? Write today's date in here and describe your life now.

2. Now go forward two years (or whatever suits you) and look back to today. Write down what you want by that time for your personal life. Then go forward five years (or so) and look back to today. Write down the additional changes you will have made.

   +2 yrs

   +5 yrs

3. Am I now at my peak performance in relationships with

Immediate family members?	Yes	No
Extended family members?	Yes	No

Friends?	Yes	No
Relevant associations such as schools, clubs, etc.?	Yes	No
Personal health?	Yes	No
Other (such as work)?	Yes	No

4. What are the key areas above that I should improve to meet my future goals?

   + 2 yrs

   + 5 yrs

5. What changes, processes and skills must I take on board to reach those objectives?

6. Now a simple vision statement for the future as to what you plan to provide for family and personal associates

and how well you are going to do it. Note that your vision statement should be broad enough to allow for an expansion of your needs and precise enough to remind you of your ownership of your future.

First write down six to eight words or phrases that describe your life and relationships as you want them to be in the future. Then write your vision statement sentence using those words, until you are happy with the result.

Your vision statement:

Don't forget to revise all your plans, as above, as often as your life, and life around you changes.

As in your business plan, the key points of your personal plan are:
- Be realistic, go with the truth. If times are tough out there, plan for that. If times are good, put funds away for when the tough times come again, as they always do.
- Be congruent. Make sure your plans pull together in a timely way to common and realistic goals.

- Be relevant. Be aware of the changing patterns of your life, and adapt to them.
- Involve all those affected by your personal plans, including family members and close associates. They know so much that you need to know but they may not tell you until you ask.
- Be flexible. Change your plans if the world changes around you. Do not wait or be 'too busy' to see the future. Read widely, attend relevant seminars and conferences, seek out specialists for their advice. Continue to involve family and friends. Consider setting up a personally chosen Board of Advisers to help you on key issues.

'It was such a lovely day I thought it was a pity to get up.'
W. Somerset Maugham (1874–1965)

■ ■ ■

Now for case studies, so that you can put it all together with Growth Skill 12.

GROWTH SKILL 12
PUT IT ALL TOGETHER USING CASE STUDIES

'Almost everyone who has become a great success in our society has been willing to take risks, and when they failed, were willing to try again and again and again.'
W Mitchell

Through this book I have mentioned most of these cases by way of example, but now I will give a full account to show the Growth Skills in action.

While working with the Inter-Continental Hotel Group in Melbourne in the 1970s, I saw what can happen when the three-month contact cycle is no longer followed. I had been very successful in building the sales of room nights into the Inter-Continental hotels worldwide, but was then taken off my sales calling pattern and put onto a research/training project.

This kept me in the office for several months, during which time I kept track of the room night sales that were coming in, regardless of my non-appearance. For three months the bookings kept at exactly the same high number of room nights and then in the fourth month fell faster than they had risen in the whole of the previous year! We lost more than we had gained.

Another international hotel group had mounted a sales campaign and the travel consultants had given up expecting to see me ever again . . . so they gave the business to the person who did show up. All that hard work disappeared virtually overnight. Loyalty lasts only with continuous follow-up. Get in there and stay there.

I had been successful in building the room nights because of reward and recognition and good systems, plus of course a good product.

This is how I did it: I kept track of the room night sales from each travel agent in Melbourne. At the end of each month, I went to the top-selling four and thanked each person for their support, offering chocolates.

I started with the Manager of the office, then on to the international travel staff and across to the receptionist. I also gave chocolates to the staff on local room night sales as they helped fill the Melbourne hotel.

I knew that in due course the receptionist and the local selling staff would move up to international travel consulting—and guess which hotel group they would then favour?

When there was a change in hotel information, I updated their Inter-Continental information book for the travel consultants.

I took the top-selling groups to lunch at the Melbourne hotel. I imported huge bunches of orchids from Singapore at New Year and just when everyone was feeling bored and lousy on the second of January, I would walk in with armloads of beautiful flowers, inviting the travel staff to take not one, but a handful.

Known as the 'orchid and chocolate lady,' I saw the outstanding effect these activities had, but only so long as the momentum was maintained. As you have read, we lost more in that fourth month than we had gained in a year.

'Thank God kids never mean well.'
Lily Tomlin

Over a year of my life with Saatchi & Saatchi Hong Kong was devoted to promoting the Pampers disposable diaper. The client, Procter & Gamble, wanted to be market leader and at that time had a 13 per cent market share. In Hong Kong there were around one hundred and twenty thousand mothers with babies of a diapering age.

We set ourselves the target of finding about one hundred

thousand families and putting all their details into the computer, thus creating a database of mothers and babies.

An all-out campaign was mounted. We used radio, TV and press to advise mothers that if they bought the Pampers product, trimmed the picture of baby's face off the pack (as proof of purchase) and sent in that with the coupon and their full name and address, we would send them a very attractive refund.

Interestingly, radio advertising with a male voice announcing the offer drew almost double the response of two female voices chatting about the offer.

'Never invest in anything that eats or needs repairing.'
Billy Rose
(1899–1966)

It seems that the reason men's voices are used more successfully in advertising is that as children we were constantly nagged at by our mothers. If we were really naughty, it was, 'Wait until your father comes home'. When he did there was a loud bellow and a lot of roaring.

Hence we listen to the male voice of authority and ignore the female nagging voice. The results of this advertising campaign seemed to prove the point that mothers, fathers and children are the same all over the world.

As the names and family details came into the computerised database, we used a promotional technique in which these mothers were invited to fill in the form we mailed to them, with the names of other mothers, for a cash reward.

In sales promotion this is known as 'Friend Get a Friend' or in this case, 'Mother Get a Mother'.

For our next activity we invited mothers to 'write their own cheque', in which they could claim refunds of up to $HKD100 for multiple purchases of the disposable diaper. This was highly successful and generated more names for the database.

Back to the media. We tested *T.V. Week* and *Motherhood and Childcare* for a major advertising campaign. *T.V. Week* was about one-third the cost of *Motherhood and Childcare* and gave us about double the response.

The cost/benefit analysis gave us the guideline for future advertising decisions.

The next stage was to go into hospitals and meet with new mothers. We decided to have a gift box for mothers containing long-term price discounts on the Pampers diaper and also on a face and body cream for the mother. (This product, Oil of Ulan/Olay, was manufactured by another Procter & Gamble company.)

The single-minded proposition for the gift box was: 'To see me is to want me'.

Our professional hospital visitors would carry the gift box as they walked around the maternity wards. Hong Kong mothers love blonde, blue-eyed babies and it was this motif that we used on the gift pack. Truly, to see it was to want it. The mothers were delighted with the pack, the offers and the information inside. Again, up went the numbers in the database.

Next we arranged to be in the centres where the babies' births were registered. Free samples with discount coupons were distributed and again there were further increases in the database names.

Additionally, the company supported pre-natal and post-natal classes, and more names were collected. We were approaching the target of 100,000 names by now.

Here's how I wrote up the process as a case study outline:

Product: Pampers disposable diaper.

Need: To make this brand the leading disposable diaper in Hong Kong.

'The reason why grandparents and grandchildren get along so well is that they have a common enemy.'
Sam Levenson
(1911–1980)

Activities:

1. Obtain the names of 100,000 mothers of infants up to three years through continuous in-store, hospital, birth registry and pre- and post-natal clinic promotions, plus continuous advertising in relevant, tested magazines and on radio and TV.

   Special offers required the mothers to apply with full name and home address details for the item (for both Pampers and the Oil of Ulan/Olay face and body lotion).

2. Form a 'Baby Club' and contact those mothers by mail on a three-monthly cycle, leading them to an educated understanding of the product and the need to move up to the next size each three months, as the baby grew.

Results: Pampers' market share grew from 13 per cent to 32 per cent in the first year, an increase of US$19 million in sales.

The demand for the product was such that market share would have been 52 per cent (a US$42 million increase) but the factory was unable to supply. I noted that another reason for the shortage of product in Hong Kong was that it was being sold on the black market in Taiwan, a country in which we were not promoting it at all. While not what we had in mind, it was certainly a compliment to our work!

On to London, where I joined MSL, a Saatchi-owned executive recruitment company. MSL had been market leader in their twenty-five years in business, but had grown a little complacent and had lost market share to more aggressive, innovative companies. Using the Saatchi three-month (or less) cycle, we went to work changing their image and market position. Here is the brief case study:

Product: Executive search, advertised selection and recruitment advertising.

Need: To revamp image from old and established to proactive, innovative, forward-thinking.

Activities:

1. Analysed existing client base and found that all were small-to-middle-sized companies. Further research indicated a fear of approaching the big companies as staff felt insecure talking to the gods of industry. The company agreed that this could be overcome with training.

   A target list of 400 major companies and 600 relevant executives was created from in-house focused research on what the current best clients had in common.

2. I then wrote a survey on 'Recruitment Issues of the 1990s' in which there were 29 significant items, including job-sharing, benefits for part-timers, maternity/paternity leave, child care, superannuation rights, training needs, effective performance reviews.

   Launched results at a lunch at the Savoy. Out of the 500 distributed, 350 major companies had filled in the surveys.

3. From these survey results we formed breakfast working parties in the MSL boardroom where those interested could share experiences and solutions to recruitment concerns and policies. Approximately one hundred and twenty human resources people attended per month.

4. Open Days every three months brought these and many other senior executives into the MSL offices to review processes such as psychological appraisals, team role models, the recruitment advertising creative processes—

> 'The intelligent man finds almost everything ridiculous, the sensible man hardly anything.'
> **Goethe**
> **(1794–1833)**

and, of course, to meet the staff.

5. Held half-day workshops for senior corporate executives, with major speakers such as Professor Charles Handy and Sir John Harvey-Jones. Attended to capacity. Participation offered at cost to ensure high level of attendance.

Results: Many significant new accounts were won. One senior executive commented that he had never heard of our company before—and now he was having nightmares about us!

On to New York on assignment with a company (IMCOR) that was in contract management. With this service, executives are leased out temporarily to corporations in need of a senior person quickly, to take up an opportunity or fix a problem.

Product: A contract management/interim executive service supplying senior executives on temporary assignments across America.

Need: To install a regular, relentless contact system to add to existing networking by the four partners.

Activities:

1. Identified commonalities of existing client base. From this defined further prospects and established a database of eight thousand companies across America. In this instance the most likely users of the service were small-to-medium-sized companies, as large corporations already had an over-supply of senior executives.

2. Corporate literature was redesigned and rewritten. Colours used were royal blue (to look solid, stable, secure and 'here forever' in spite of only having been in

business for three years), with a large block of white copy (in contrast) down the right-hand side of the front cover, explaining the service and its uses. (You will remember that when the copy is placed on the right-hand side, it goes directly through to the left-hand, analytical side of the brain. The company is therefore perceived as being solid, stable, secure and here to stay.)

A regular, relentless contact pattern was established within the three-month cycle, in which the large, new, royal blue brochure (versus the old, small, cream one) was mailed with a covering letter. Then came phone follow-up for appointments for the partners.

The special offer was a full credit of interim fees against the permanent fees, if the contract/interim manager became a full-time employee. This happened so often that it was promoted as 'executive tryout'. The deduction of the contract fees from the permanent placement cost was therefore a very significant offer. It allowed all parties to recognise that a permanent placement was possible, even to working out the costs beforehand.

3. Identified relevant conferences for niche markets, such as the financial sector. Achieved high visibility at these conferences through a planned program of sponsorship and contact before, during and after the meeting dates, advising of the contract management/interim services. Committed to three conferences, two months apart, to implant the product message.

Results: Combined with highly successful PR activities, the regular, relentless marketing program raised the company's profile to that of market leader in America.

Acceptance of appointments with the partners reached a

'Don't be humble—you are not that great.'
Golda Meir
(1898–1978)

ratio as high as seven out of ten by the third round of mailing and phone contact, as the product was new and there was a great need for temporary senior executives. IMCOR was then able to consider franchising their service across America and beyond.

Now back to Australia, where my client, Thomas Cook, had a traditional base of older English-background clients. Thomas Cook was aware that their sales were now predominantly in air travel, although they had previously been very strong in cruising and coach tours.

Product: High profile travel agent, with travellers' cheque division.

Owned by the Midland Bank UK at that time.

Needs:

1. Thomas Cook had been pre-eminent in cruising sales but had slipped back over the years and wished to regain its position.
2. Thomas Cook had a large base of older clients and wanted to expand into the youth area. A broader base would protect it against the ageing of its traditional clients and increase its range of product sales.

Activities:

1. We researched favourite travel activities of the youth market and cruising showed up strongly. As a result Thomas Cook mounted a campaign with Sitmar, centred around their Bankstown travel shop. This area has a considerable number of young people who were easily accessible in the town square at lunchtime and through their office jobs.

2. Travel staff dressed in nautical clothes distributed invitations to the staff of Bankstown businesses to attend a free Sitmar disco at a local venue. The tickets were available only through Thomas Cook's Bankstown travel office. Names, addresses and phone numbers of the applicants were captured at that time.

   The invitations were particularly attractive, with a colourful cocktail drink parasol neatly attached to the outside, as well as excellent special offers if bookings on Sitmar were made within six months.

3. The disco was run by Thomas Cook and Sitmar staff and a top disc jockey. The evening reflected the fun of the Sitmar experience and was attended by around five hundred young employed people in Bankstown.

Result: The Bankstown office became the top-selling Thomas Cook office for Sitmar and P & O cruises, plus Royal Viking. Parents of the youth who had attended the disco now booked their P & O and Royal Viking cruises through the Bankstown office. Children and friends bounded aboard for more of the Sitmar experience. The local newspaper covered the event well, from our initial contact with a press release.

Follow-up contact included telephone research as to what had most pleased the young people attending. Results showed that they had loved the fine quality of the invitation, were delighted with the presence of the bouncers whom we hired for the occasion and felt very safe, secure and welcomed, so they would cruise with Sitmar at any time. No one had any complaints.

It is interesting that the quality of the bouncers came up so often. In doing youth promotions, it seems very important to give them good, safe fun in a large crowd.

'If they could put one man on the moon, why can't they put them all.'
Unknown

We did follow-up mailings within three months to those who had attended, to remind them of the special offers. Another follow-up letter and brochure went out again in another three months to those who had not yet booked, and they were contacted regularly thereafter with other special offers.

The problem with the youth market is that addresses change more often than with older people and far more mail was returned. However, the young grow older and become more stable, book higher-price ticket items and become the senior citizens of the future. Moral of the story: bring them in young.

Now an exciting experience further down-under in the new South Africa. In Johannesburg an ABSA bank branch was losing 100 clients a week. My job was to be their education officer. Always ready for the new, I spent one of the most interesting periods of my life working with the staff there to turn the branch around. Here's the good news!

Product: Banking

Needs: Stop the rush away from the branch. With one hundred or so clients a week moving on, through emigration **and** dissatisfaction, we could change only the latter reason. Training had to be in the evening, because the day's work had to be done, daily!

Activities: First the staff read about the skills outlined in this book and then night after night we worked through them, beginning with the SWOT analysis so that we could identify the key issues for the branch.

Like virtually all companies I have worked with around the

world, one of the major problems is that the staff were not involved in the business or marketing plans, and therefore felt they had no control over the success or failure of the branch.

At the end of the study period came the big question, 'Of all the things we have reviewed together, what would you like to spend more time on?' I asked.

The answer surprised me. 'Business plans and marketing plans'. When I queried their choice, they replied that they spent most of their working life on family banking needs and did not really understand how businesses worked. They therefore hesitated to contact the business community in their area.

We then did a business plan together to grow the branch, and marketing plans to promote specific products.

Next: The staff decided to target personal loans—a product of which they previously sold around two a month. They set themselves targets: a minimum of 20 personal loans for the month, maximum 40 loans.

The staff contacted the community through advertising in local papers, household letterbox drops, posters and information in the branch and through talking directly to staff in the regional office and other banks, plus friends, family, relatives and of course, clients.

The result: Sixty-five personal loans were signed up in one month. 'We're geniuses!' they said to me with glee. And indeed they were.

More results: The staff went on to target nursery school parents to take out educational funds for their children, then into old-age homes to help clients too old to travel to better invest their funds.

They hand-wrote cards to people whose fixed deposits had

'Warning to all personnel. Firings will continue until morale improves.'
Unknown

passed their due dates and hence were earning no interest. Having previously sent official letters and phoned, they were amazed at the near 100 per cent response to the handwritten cards. It seemed the only clients who did not respond were those whose addresses had changed.

Final result: A branch that had been losing around one hundred clients a week through emigration and dissatisfaction started **putting on over** one hundred clients per week! Encouraged by training and incentives they went on to earn a good bonus—just in time for Christmas.

They had taken responsibility for defining their promotional activities, for writing the copy, designing the layout and even walked their talk by delivering the household letterbox drops.

For myself, I learned that empowering people to create their own destiny is all about having the business skills to define the direction, make the decisions, and get on with making it happen. People do truly want to work well and be effective; they only need the skills to make it happen.

MAGIC MOMENTS OF CUSTOMER CARE

Just occasionally something unexpectedly excellent happens and because of it, you remember with pleasure the person and the company they represent forever.

For instance, in London I had a very pleasant meal at the Dorchester Hotel, and the bill was more than reasonable. I commented to the waiter that I thought I had been undercharged and he replied: 'If you have, Madam, it has been our pleasure.' Mine too.

When I returned to Australia from New York, I wanted to test-drive the (then) new Mazda Astina hatch back. Living on

'When I saw a sign on the freeway that said,"Los Angeles 445 miles," I said to myself. "I've got to get out of this lane".'
Franklin Ajaye

Sydney's Upper North Shore at the time, I somehow managed to ring the distant, outer west Blacktown showroom. Yet they offered to bring the car over for a test drive. All the way from Blacktown?

I expressed my surprise later to the salesperson, Daniel Eagen, and he said that since Blacktown was so far from everywhere, they had decided that the only way to sell to prospects was in their own homes.

Yes, I did buy their Mazda. Their service and care were excellent all the way.

The point of these two stories, is of course, that it is not hard to stand out in the crowd. If you want to be a market leader in your field, it only takes common sense and some gentle good manners.

The hotel story is exceptional in that the waiter took the initiative not to worry about a small amount of money and did it so politely. The Mazda story is one of rare common sense that turned a disadvantage into a selling point.

Compare that experience with this: the same day that I rang Mazda at Blacktown, I test-drove a Nissan nearby. The sales manager told me that I had to make up my mind by the weekend as the prices went up on Saturday! This is the oldest sales technique in the book, so guaranteed that I would not buy.

And here is a magic vet story. I moved from one suburb to another, and in the shift my dog got run over. Too far from her usual vet to transport her damaged body, I rang them for a referral, which they gave me for a vet just nearby. She was very well looked after and lived to be more wary of cars. The magic moment? The previous vet rang **daily** to see how she was getting on.

Want to know more? Turn over for some highly recommended books.

'The trouble with loving is that pets don't last long enough and people last too long.'
Unknown

RECOMMENDED READING

To help you on your way with more in-depth knowledge on achieving success in your own business, I put together the following list of top-selling books in each of the subjects covered in this book, plus some extras that may be well worth your time. Good luck and good reading! Thank you for joining me on this voyage.

Advertising Skills:

Albert C. Book & C. Dennis Schuck. *The Fundamentals of Copy & Layout*, NTC, 1988

Claude C. Hopkins. *My Life in Advertising*, NTC Books, 1987

Herschell Gordon Lewis. *The Art of Writing Copy*, Prentice Hall, 1989

David Ogilvy. *Ogilvy on Advertising*, Pan Books, 1983

Business Plans:

William S. Birnbaum. *If Your Strategy is So Terrific, How Come It Doesn't Work?* Amacom, 1990

Ron Johnson. *The 24-hour Business Plan*, Hutchinson, 1990

Kenichi Ohmae. *The Mind of the Strategist*, McGraw-Hill, 1982

Business Writing:

Laura Brill. *Business Writing Quick and Easy*, Amacom, 1989

Thelma Mansell. *How to Write Business Letters and Reports*, Pitman, 1990

Gladys Snodgrass & Elizabeth Murphy. *Letter Writing Simplified*, Pitman, 1986

Colour—Its Effect on You and in Business:

Dr Max Luscher, translated by Ian Scott. *The Luscher Color Test*, Washington Square Press/Pocket Books, 1987

Kenneth H. Mills and Judith E. Paul. *Applied Visual Merchandising*, Prentice Hall, 1988

Contact Management:

Lee Boyan. *Successful Cold Calling*, Amacom, 1989

Customer Service:

William H. Davidow & Bro. Uttal. *Total Customer Service*,
    Harper Perennial, 1990

Carl Sewell. *Customers for Life*, Pocket Books, 1990

Richard C. Whitely. *The Customer Driven Company. Moving from Talk
    to Action*, Century Business, 1991

V. Zeithami. *Delivering Quality Service*, Free Press, 1989

Ron Zemke and Chip R. Bell. *Managing Knock Your Socks Off Service*,
    Amacom, 1992

Direct Marketing:

Ian Kennedy & Bryce Courtenay. *The Power of One to One*, Margaret Gee
    Publishing, Australia, 1995 and Zebra, South Africa, 1996

Drayton Bird. *Commonsense Direct Marketing*, Kogan Page, 1988

Charles Mallory. *Direct Mail Magic*, Crisp Publications, 1991

Bob Stone. *Successful Direct Marketing*, NTC, 1989

Management Skills:

Stephen R. Covey. *The 7 Habits of Highly Effective People*,
    The Business Library, 1992

Peter Senge. *The Fifth Discipline. The Art and Practice of the Learning
    Organisation*, Random House, 1991

Michael J.S. Spendolini. *The Benchmarking Book*, Amacom, 1992

Marketing Plans:

Laura M. Dirks & Sally H. Daniel. *Marketing Without Mystery—a Practical
    Guide to Writing a Marketing Plan*, Amacom, 1991

Market Research:

Michael Baker. *Research for Marketing*, MacMillan, 1991

Paul Hague & Peter Jackson. *Marketing Research in Practice*, Page, 1992

Neurolinguistics:

Johnson, Kerry. *Selling with NLP. The revolutionary new sales techniques that will double your volume*, Positive Paperbacks, Nicholas Brealey Publishing, London, 1994

Byron Lewis & Frank Pucelik. *Magic of NLP Demystified*, Metamorphous Press, 1990

Psychological Profiling:

Isabel Briggs Myers. *Gifts Differing*, Consulting Psychologists Press, 1980

Public Relations:

Roger Hayward. *All About Public Relations*, McGraw-Hill, 1991

Tymson & Sherman. *The Australian Public Relations Manual*, Millennium Books, 1990

Sales Promotion:

Julian Cummins. *Sales Promotion*, Kogan Page, 1989

Self-Promotion:

Victoria Seitz. *Your Executive Image—the Art of Self Packaging*, Bob Adams Inc, 1991

Selling Skills:

Mack Hanan. *Consultative Selling*, Amacom, 1990

Michael Hewitt-Gleeson. *NewSell*, Wrightbooks, 1990

Robert B. Miller et al. *Strategic Selling*, Warner Books, 1985

Larry Wilson with Hersch Wilson. *Changing the Game*: *The New Way to Sell*, Fireside, 1988

Small Business Management:

T.F. Gaffney. *First Steps in Small Business*, Butterworths, 1990

Telephone and telemarketing:

Lloyd C. Finch. *Telephone Courtesy & Customer Service*,
Crisp Publications, 1990

Julie Freestone & Janet Brusse. *Telemarketing Basics*,
Crisp Publications, 1989

Caroline Greewich. *The Fun Factor*, McGraw Hill, Sydney 1997

Time Management:

Stephen R. Covey. *First Things First*, The Business Library, 1993

Merrill E. Douglas, Donna N. Douglas. *Manage Your Time, Your Work,
Yourself*, Amacom, 1985

William Oncken Jr. *Managing Management Time*, Prentice Hall, 1984

D. Scott. *Time Management and the Telephone*, Crisp Publications, 1987

INDEX